A Year With Mary

Elizabeth Ruth Obbard is novice-mistress of a Carmelite community in Norfolk. She is the author of numerous published books including *The History and Spirituality of Walsingham*, *See How I Love You*, *A Walsingham Prayer Book* and *To Live is to Pray* which are published by the Canterbury Press.

A Year With Mary

*Prayers and Readings for the
Christian Year*

Elizabeth Ruth Obbard

CANTERBURY
PRESS
Norwich

© Elizabeth Ruth Obbard 1998

First published in 1998 by The Canterbury Press
Norwich (a publishing imprint of Hymns Ancient &
Modern Limited, a registered charity),
St Mary's Works, St Mary's Plain,
Norwich, Norfolk, NR3 3BH

British Library Cataloguing in Publication Data

A catalogue record for this book is available
from the British Library

ISBN 1-85311-240-2

Typeset by Rowland Phototypesetting,
Bury St Edmunds, Suffolk
Printed in Great Britain by
Biddles Ltd, Guildford and King's Lynn

For Robin and Jan Sayer
with gratitude

Contents

Foreword

In her book *Dead Man Walking*, Sr Helen Prejean, who has exercised an apostolate to people on Death Row in the USA, tells of watching before the Blessed Sacrament one night with the father of one of her executed murderer's victims. It is warm and dark and silent. Together Helen, Lloyd the father, and Louie, Helen's brother, reach for their rosaries. In the round beads passing through their hands they remember the death of Jesus, his agony and crucifixion. Meanwhile the beads continue their progress, being held ... letting go ... as the prayer of the rosary continues ... with Mary, with Jesus ... holding mutely on to love, love that alone is solid and lasting.

In meditating on the sorrowful mysteries Lloyd has again and again to hold and then let go of his own murdered son. It is done through the old familiar prayers, and in the company of a mother who also lost her Son and found him again at the Resurrection.

Mary is the one who is the familiar companion of our own lives. She has felt as we feel, she has lost and found her Child, she is with us day and night, a gentle, motherly/ sisterly presence, as she has been to countless Christians down through the ages of faith.

This book then has nothing essentially new to say about Mary. It is merely a reliving of the Christian year with a woman loved and revered through the centuries, a collection which honours Mary, 'blessed for her believing'. To each one who turns to her she offers a special relationship that is as old as Christianity itself. Men and women have cried to her in their need and sung with her in their joy. They have seen in her a model of the perfect disciple and a companion on their journey of faith.

Mary is the one to whom people have turned at those two moments of life which alone matter – NOW, and the hour of death. This book is an invitation to do just that.

Advent

Advent is the Marian season *par excellence*. It is a time of darkness, of silence, of waiting and preparing for the birth of Christ, just as Mary waited silently, cherishing the unborn child she carried in her womb.

We realize now the importance of this embryonic stage of development. A child who is wanted, who is loved even when hidden, is already drawing from its mother a basic sense of life's goodness. With what happiness must Mary have waited and prepared for the moment of Jesus' birth. How she must have shared this precious time with Joseph, with her family and friends, and how she must have folded herself inwards silently as she nourished the child from her own substance, feeling him grow and move and respond to her singing.

Advent is a time to spend waiting in expectation with Mary, letting the darkness of winter speak to us of life unseen but sure. It is a time to be filled with trust in the advent of God, who comes to be with us as one of us.

'May the God who gives us peace make you completely his' are the words that meet us from Scripture on the threshold of the first Sunday of Advent. It would be good to focus on that word *completely* as the new liturgical year begins.

A candle burns, and if it remains alight and shining for the whole time, it is consumed completely. If it is frequently lit and then extinguished again after a short while, it burns only down the centre. The excess wax must then be pared away, otherwise the flame is stifled and the wick drowns.

This season begins with the single light of the first Advent candle. It ends on the feast of the Purification when we celebrate Mary bringing her Son to the Temple, the Light of the nations and the glory of Israel; then all is ablaze with flames of welcome.

To be *completely* God's is to be turned to him so as to be *always* burning, *always* shining; every part of ourselves consumed in his service and the service of our brothers and sisters. There is nothing whatever kept back 'just for me', nor do I shine only 'occasionally' or 'when the Spirit moves me', but *always* and *completely*.

A candle may not give out much light when compared with the darkness around it, but it gives all it can for as long as it can. And, like a candle, our life too is to be consumed before the face of Christ.

Mary was totally God's – all his – body and soul. She embodied the ages of Israel's waiting, longing, praying; like a single candle burning bravely in the darkness, that light was faithful Israel surrounded by pagan nations. And because in the darkness Mary, the faithful daughter of Sion, shone with radiance, a radiance that was never extinguished by any sin or infidelity however slight, she was able to bear the Light that enlightens the whole world, the Sun of justice, Christ our God.

Adorn your bridal chamber, O Sion,
and receive Christ the King.
Greet Mary, the gate of heaven, with loving embrace;
for she bears the King of Glory, the new Light.
There stands the Virgin, in her arms the Son

begotten before the Daystar,
all light because she bears the Light.

Antiphon for 2 February

With Mary we are called to be light-bearers. So let us encourage one another, not quenching the wavering flame when we see faults and weaknesses, but lovingly trimming the wick and removing excess wax so that the flame can burn brightly once more.

In Advent we think of Mary waiting for the birth of her child. We think of the Church waiting for Christ to come again in glory. And each one of us waits and longs for redemption, for the new birth, new life, new hope that is symbolized in a newborn child – light in darkness, Spring in the middle of Winter.

It is for us to wait, with Mary, burning and shining, with complete trust in the Lord's coming; *completely* consumed, like a candle that burns continually before him.

* * *

Sing for joy, O heavens, and exult, O earth;
break forth, O mountains, into singing!
For the Lord has comforted his people,
and will have compassion on his suffering ones.
But Zion said, 'The Lord has forsaken me,
my Lord has forgotten me.'
Can a woman forget her nursing child,
or show no compassion for the child of her womb?
Even these may forget, yet I will not forget you.
See, I have inscribed you on the palms of my hands.

Isaiah 49:13–16a

A voice cries out:
'In the wilderness prepare the way of the Lord,
make straight in the desert a highway for our God.'

Isaiah 40:3

I wait for the Lord, my soul waits,
and in his word I hope;
my soul waits for the Lord
more than those who watch for the morning,
more than those who watch for the morning.

Psalm 130:5–6

The virginal quality which, for want of a better word, I call emptiness, is the beginning of contemplation.

It is not a formless emptiness, a void without meaning; on the contrary it has a shape, a form given to it by the purpose for which it was intended.

It is emptiness like the hollow in the reed, the narrow riftless emptiness which can only have one destiny: to receive the piper's breath and to utter the song that is in his heart. It is emptiness like the hollow in the cup, shaped to receive water or wine.

It is emptiness like that of the bird's nest, built in a warm round ring to receive the little bird.

The pre-Advent emptiness of Our Lady's purposeful virginity was indeed like those three things.

She was the reed through which the Eternal Love was to be piped as a shepherd's song.

She was the flower-like chalice into which the purest water of humanity was to be poured, mingled with wine, changed to the crimson blood of love, and lifted up in sacrifice.

She was the warm nest rounded to the shape of humanity to receive the Divine Little Bird.

The whole process of contemplation through imitation of our Lady can be gone through, in the first place, with just that simple purpose of regaining the virgin mind, and as we go on in the attempt we shall find that over and over again there is a new emptying process; it is a thing that has to be done in contemplation as often as the earth has to be sifted and the field ploughed for seed.

Caryll Houselander

The Church has willed – and what is more just? – that the liturgy of Advent should be full of the thought of the Blessed Virgin; she continually makes us sing the divine fruitfulness of the Virgin, a wonderful fruitfulness that throws nature into astonishment . . .

There is something truly ineffable about the Virgin during those days. She lived in an intimate union with the Infant God whom she bore within her. The soul of Jesus was, by the Beatific Vision, plunged in the divine light; this light radiated upon his Mother. In the sight of the angels, Mary truly appeared as 'a woman clothed with the sun', all irradiated with heavenly brightness, all shining with the light of her Son . . .

Let us humbly ask her to make us enter into her dispositions. She will hear our prayer; we shall have the immense joy of seeing Christ born anew within our hearts by the communication of a more abundant grace, and we shall be enabled, like the Virgin, although in a lesser measure, to understand the truth of these words of St John: 'The Word was God . . . and the Word was made flesh and dwelt among us, and we saw his glory . . . full of grace

and truth . . . And of his fullness we have all received, grace
upon grace.'

Dom Marmion

Father, All-powerful and ever-living God,
we do well always and everywhere to give you thanks
through Jesus Christ our Lord.
His future coming was proclaimed by the prophets.
The virgin mother bore him in her womb with love
    beyond all telling.
John the Baptist was his herald
and made him known when at last he came.
In his love Christ has filled us with joy
as we prepare to celebrate his birth,
so that when he comes he may find us watching in
    prayer,
our hearts filled with wonder and praise.

Advent Preface from the Roman Missal

O true Light, our Lord God,
who from the depths of your heart
have voiced the saving Word.
We pray to you;
as wondrously you descended
into the pure womb of the Virgin Mary,
grant us, your servants,
to await with joy the glorious Nativity.

Scroll of Ravenna,
Fourth–Fifth centuries

Loving mother of the Redeemer,
open door to heaven and star of the sea,
come quickly to the aid of your people,
fallen indeed, yet seeking to stand again.
To nature's astonishment
you were the mother of the holy Creator
without ceasing to be a virgin,
and heard Gabriel's greeting of *Ave*.
Have pity on us sinners.

Advent antiphon to the Virgin
Hermann Contractus, 1054

O God, who in the virgin's womb, with wondrous art
have made a holy dwelling in the flesh;
come, you righteous One, come quickly,
and, according to the ancient promise
ransom humanity from its plight.
To you let there rise up the praise
worthy of so great a love,
and to us be given eternal salvation.

Scroll of Ravenna

The Virgin, weighed
with the Word of God,
comes down the road:
if only you'll shelter her.

St John of the Cross

December 8

The Immaculate Conception

The Immaculate Conception is a dogma not easy to speak about in a way that touches our ordinary lives. The language of poetry and symbolism, such as the Liturgy of the feast provides, is far richer in expressing the inexhaustible mystery. To be 'conceived without taint of original sin' sounds dry, whereas at Mass and the Divine Office we are confronted with wonderful texts on Mary's rejoicing, her being clothed in salvation, made holy by the robe of God around her. She sings from the heart her *Magnificat* of gratitude and praise for God's goodness and choice, which are totally unmerited.

The scriptural foundation for the Immaculate Conception is in the second chapter of St Luke's Gospel where Mary is greeted as being 'full of grace'; that is, something has been done for her before the moment of the Annunciation. She is already a 'graced' woman when the angel greets her.

It is Luke who gives us the familiar image of the Virgin venerated by the Church. Without his Gospel would there have been such veneration? Would there be warrant for it? But pause – Luke is not the originator of this Mary, as though he has used his imagination like a novelist, creating her out of the bare fact that Jesus had a mother called Mary while the rest is no more than conjecture.

Luke sees himself as a careful preserver of tradition: what has been delivered and handed on by eye-witnesses.

He is taking up material gathered after careful enquiry, that his readers may 'know the truth'.

While the Gospel of John seems to put Mary in a symbolic womanly role, rather than in a personal one, Luke shows her as the perfect disciple. The Annunciation is *for us*; the *Magnificat* is *our* song. We too have to ponder in our hearts 'all these things' about Jesus in order to extract their meaning.

Mary, in her whole person, is the Christian as he or she is meant to be. Luke shows her as a woman who is holy, full of grace, one in whom God was able to have his way. Thus we have in Mary a living message, a living portrayal, of ourselves and our destiny.

We know little about the details of Mary's life, but we know all that matters. Luke contrasts her with Zechariah, who is also the recipient of an angelic message. Zechariah is a priest who ministers in Jerusalem, the centre of Israelite cultic worship. Mary, on the other hand, is a mere girl from pagan Galilee; she does not even have the dignity of marriage or ancestry (that comes through Joseph). She has no priestly antecedents. She is not approached in the temple but in the setting of the ordinary world of home. The event is secret, whereas all get to know of Zechariah's encounter with the angel at the altar of incense.

Zechariah and Elizabeth have prayed for a son; now their prayer is answered. God has heard them and rewarded their fidelity. They are the very best of the Old Testament 'type', yet this is as far as the Old Testament can go. Mary, by contrast, is the recipient of grace, unmerited and unasked. All is God's work from first to last. She is addressed as 'highly favoured one'. What has she done to deserve this accolade? Precisely nothing! She is favoured because of what *God* has done for her.

No doubt Mary observed the Law like Zechariah, but that is not the point. Her centre is *grace*. *God* favours, *God* gives, *God* acts and loves and cherishes. Mary simply responds, takes the Word into herself, lets it fructify.

But does this choice of grace take Mary, or us, out of the human situation? We can easily confuse 'being without sin' with 'not being quite human'. That would be a gross mistake. We can think that sin is in the human condition *per se*; in having bodily needs and instincts and emotions, which, unless they conform to a certain pattern are 'sinful' because they can make us *feel* sinful. But they are not sinful in themselves. Sin is in the will. For all we know, Mary may have had a difficult temperament which meant that she did not *feel* holy at all! What we *do* know is that Mary never chose against God, never chose to offend him, never refused his love.

Mary demonstrates that in holiness and surrender we are most fulfilled and completed. Sin makes us less, not more, human. God never goes back on his choice and his love for us, but we can fail to reciprocate.

If our daily living is not making us more and more Christ-like, more and more ready to respond to our own unique vocation as Mary responded to hers, we are failing the Lord.

Grace is the love of God, freely given to us, moulding us into the pattern of Christ. Surely this feast is then a feast on which to rejoice in the God who is *our* Saviour as he is Mary's; the God who has called and graced us beyond all imagining.

* * *

You are the glory of Jerusalem, you are the great boast of Israel, you are the great pride of our nation.

Judith 15:9

The Immaculate Conception

I will greatly rejoice in the Lord,
my whole being shall exult in my God;
for he has clothed me with the garments of salvation,
he has covered me with the robe of righteousness,
as a bridegroom decks himself with a garland,
and as a bride adorns herself with her jewels . . .
You shall be a crown of beauty in the hand of the
*   Lord,*
and a royal diadem in the hand of your God.
You shall no more be termed Forsaken,
and your land shall no more be termed Desolate;
but you shall be called My Delight Is In Her,
and your land Married.

Isaiah 61:10–11; 62:3–4

Blessed be the God and Father of our Lord Jesus Christ,
who has blessed us in Christ with every spiritual blessing
in the heavenly places, just as he chose us in Christ before
the foundation of the world to be holy and blameless before
him in love. He destined us for adoption as his children
through Jesus Christ, according to the good pleasure of his
will, to the praise of his glorious grace that he freely
bestowed on us in the Beloved.

Ephesians 1:3–6

Mary Immaculate,
Merely a woman, yet
Whose presence, power is
Great as no goddess's
Was deemèd, dreamèd; who
This one work had to do –

Let all God's glory through,
God's glory, which would go
Thro' her and from her flow
Off, and no way but so.

Gerard Manley Hopkins

The Immaculate Conception shows that God's call is a summons to what is most individual. He establishes the beginnings in love and irrevocable fidelity to his own plan, he lays down grace as the real and comprehensive beginning, for Mary and for us . . .

And because he willed a mother for his Son, he willed her to be like his incarnate Logos himself, free in herself even before God. Consequently the first beginning of this mother is truly like the start of a real journey, where one has to find one's way. That is why the glorious beginning, rich in love and immutable, irrevocable fidelity, was, nevertheless, the beginning of a life story, an adventure, a beginning that gave rise to more than it actually contained . . .

May the blessed Virgin whose first beginning was holy and pure, pray for us, that we too may become what we are.

Karl Rahner

Calm, O maiden most pure, the wild storm of my soul,
for you alone showed yourself on earth to be
the port of all who set a course through the perils of life.
You who gave birth to the Light,
brighten, O pure Lady, the eyes of my heart.
You were given to us on earth as protection, bulwark
    and boast.
You were given to us as a tower and sure salvation,
    O maiden.

For this we no longer fear adversity,
we who devoutly glorify you.

Joseph the Studite, 832

You are all fair, O Mary, you are all fair.
The stain of original sin is not in you.
How beautiful you are,
what sweetness of delight is in your Immaculate
    Conception.

You came forth radiant as the morning star,
bearing with you the joyful tidings of salvation.
Through you, O shining portal of light,
arose the Sun of Justice, even Christ our God

As the lily among thorns,
so are you, O blessed Virgin, among the daughters of
    Adam.
Your raiment is resplendent as the dazzling snow;
your face beauteous as the sun.

In you is all hope of life and of virtue;
in you is all grace of the way and of the truth.
We run after you in the sweet attraction of your
    virtues.

You are a garden enclosed, a fountain sealed,
the Mother of God, the source of grace.
The rain is over and gone, the winter is now past,
flowers have appeared again.

In our land a voice has been heard, a most sweet
    voice:
the voice of the turtle, the voice of the dove.
Take wing, O most beautiful dove,
Arise, make haste and come.

Come, come from Libanus; come, come from Libanus.
Come, come, you shall be crowned.

J. Pothier OSB (Trans. from the Latin)

O Holy Virgin
who have begotten the Word in flesh,
bless our souls,
let us live in faithfulness,
we who at all times praise you
and proclaim you thus.
Save us, O gate of salvation;
protect us, O mother of truth;
succour the faithful who honour you.
O Immaculate,
save us from the possible, innumerable failures.
O most pure,
protect, guard and defend
those who hope in you.

Sergius of Constantinople, 638

Father,
the image of the Virgin is found in the Church.
Mary had a faith that your Spirit prepared
and a love that never knew sin,
for you kept her sinless from the first moment of her
    conception.
Trace in our actions the lines of her love,
in our hearts her readiness for faith.
Prepare once again a world for your Son.

Roman Missal

December 25

Christmas Day

Mother and Child – this is the focus of Christmas. The figures of Mary and her baby Son have graced every crib in church or home ever since St Francis first re-enacted the Christmas story at Greccio.

Christmas is a feast that touches deep chords of emotion in each one of us. It touches memories of our own childhood and early years, of other Christmases, happy or sad. We become aware of feelings of love, sweetness, tenderness which are not usually uppermost at other times, when we are adults trying to cope in an 'adult' world. At Christmas we are all children again – vulnerable, trusting, fragile. Mother and child are archetypal symbols; one does not have to be a Christian, or even religious, to appreciate and respond to what they stand for.

Christmas highlights the incarnational aspect of our lives. It tells us of God's humanity. God knows, not merely intellectually, but from the inside, what it is to be human. Jesus has had a human mother like us; he has been through life from cradle to grave. He is no God-out-there; he is Emmanuel, God-with-us. God has become flesh in a babe.

Here we have a parable of Jesus' whole life. Jesus was *always* a child, vulnerable, needy, and never more so than when helpless in the manger and stretched out on the cross. So many carols reflect this paradox: the birth in a wooden manger, the death on a wooden cross; the cry of the new-born child and the cry of the death agony; the swaddling bands of Bethlehem and the winding cloths of the grave. God has put himself at our mercy in Crib, Cross and Eucharist. We can reject, destroy, abuse him, just as some parents abuse their trusting little ones.

So Christmas carries a foreshadowing of Calvary, just as having feelings means being able to suffer and grieve as well as to know ecstatic happiness.

We can see this in Mary as we focus on her too during this celebration. On the human level, motherhood opens a woman to a new world – of pain and joy and responsibility – very different to virginity, or even marriage without children. A woman's deepest instincts are activated in motherhood. She no longer lives for herself alone but for her child. This love overrides all others. If she is put in a position where she has to choose between husband and child she will nearly always choose her child, she can do no other.

Through Mary, whether we are physically mothers or not, we come to understand, empathically, what it means to live for another. The Child in the crib is *our* Child too. Our lives are *for him*. He has placed himself at *our* mercy.

Christmas embraces our past and our present – all that we have been and all that we are – taking everything to the mystery of the babe in the manger. He is *us* in so many ways: full of potentialities that must grow, capacities for feeling pain and bliss, the whole gamut of human emotions and human experience.

Mary as mother of this Child had to learn to live for him in ways she could not possibly have known beforehand. And then she had to let him go from her to be his own person; one of the hardest lessons we all have to learn about those we love.

'One who grows in love grows in grief,' said St Catherine of Siena. Looking at the Child Jesus and his mother we glimpse our own tepidity, how we have failed to respond as we should to so much love poured out for us – God going to so much trouble to help us understand how much we are loved.

But Christmas is primarily a feast of hope. A child is always a symbol of hope – hope of new life, new joy, a new future. We can, even now, enter into the mystery of love and respond in a deeper, more selfless way.

Mary, the once barren daughter of Sion, is now the mother of many children through her Son, ourselves included. At Christmas we can place ourselves in her arms, allowing her to love us as she loved Jesus her newborn babe; or we can, with her and in her place, hold the Child and pour out our love upon the One who cannot threaten or condemn, but only give love in return.

By this Child's coming to us, touching us, we are healed, purified and transformed. He does nothing by remote control; he comes himself to be our joy and fulfilment.

If we hold this Child close, we will find, like Mary, that all becomes possible, because love makes everything easy and light.

* * *

Listen to me, you that pursue righteousness,
you that seek the Lord.
Look to the rock from which you were hewn,
and to the quarry from which you were dug.
Look to Abraham your father and to Sarah who bore
* you . . .*
For the Lord will comfort Zion;
he will comfort all her waste places,
and will make her wilderness like Eden,

her desert like the garden of the Lord;
joy and gladness will be found in her,
thanksgiving and the voice of song.

Isaiah 51:1-3

In those days a decree went out from the Emperor Augus-
tus that all the world should be registered ... Joseph also
went from the town of Nazareth in Galilee to Judea, to
the city of David called Bethlehem, because he was
descended from the house and family of David. He went
to be registered with Mary, to whom he was engaged and
who was expecting a child. While they were there, the time
came for her to deliver her child. And she gave birth to
her first-born son and wrapped him in bands of cloth, and
laid him in a manger, because there was no place for them
in the inn.

Luke 2:1-7

Although he [the Lord] was great and rich, he became
small and poor for us. He chose to be born away from
home in a stable, to be wrapped in swaddling clothes, to
be nourished by virginal milk and to lie in a manger
between an ox and an ass. Then 'there shone upon us a
day of new redemption, restoration of the past and eternal
happiness. Then through the whole world the heavens
became honey-sweet.'

Now, then, my soul,
embrace that divine manger;
press your lips upon and kiss the boy's feet.
Then in your mind
keep the shepherds' watch,

marvel at the assembling host of angels,
join in the heavenly melody,
singing with your voice and heart;
Glory to God in the highest
and on earth peace
to all those of good will.

St Bonaventure, 1274

In the body I am at Nazareth, but in the spirit I have been in Bethlehem for the past month. As I write to you I feel as though I am with Mary and Joseph beside the crib. It is good to be there. Outside are the cold and the snow, images of the world; but in the little cave, lit by the light of Jesus, it is sweet and warm and light. Father Abbot asks me what it is the Divine Child whispers to me all this month as I watch at his feet at night between his holy parents, when he comes into my arms and enters into my heart in Holy Communion. He says over and over again, 'The will of God, the will of God.' 'Behold I come. In the head of the book of life it is written that I should do your will.' This is what the beloved voice of the Divine Child gently murmurs to me.

Charles de Foucauld

No one has penetrated the mystery of Christ in its depth, except the Virgin. This mother of grace is going to form my soul so that her little child may be a living image, a striking image of her first-born, the Son of the Eternal One, the One who was the perfect praise of his Father's glory.

Bl. Elizabeth of the Trinity

Hail Mary, Star of morning,
Bright herald of the sun!
Whose light the day adorning
Revealed the Holy One.
Ere time began, through grace,
God chose you for his mother,
O pride of all our race.

Hail Mary, sweet and tender,
Your Son is God on high,
Th'eternal Father's splendour
As Scriptures testify.
Fair Maid, you brought to birth
Christ Jesus, your own Maker,
Who has no peer on earth.

German Carol

O Lady, sweetness itself,
by the visit you made to Elizabeth
into the hill country;
by her hailing you blessed,
and the fruit of your womb;
Lady, may your blessed Fruit fill my heart.
And by all you felt when he stirred within you,
Sweet Lady, bid him stir in my heart,
to serve and honour him.
O Lady, sweetness itself,
by the joy that was yours on Christmas Day,
when your sweet Son was born to you;
bid him give me the blessed birth of my Redemption.

Book of Hours, 1451

Eternal God and creator of life,
who by the coming of the birth of Christ took flesh,
we pray to you that he be full of mercy
to us, his humble servants.
He the Word, came to us from the womb of the Holy
    Virgin,
becoming flesh and dwelling among us.

Scroll of Ravenna

Grace-filled, unspotted, God-bearing Virgin,
holy your womb: Emmanuel lay in it.
You fed at your breast the food of the world.
What praise can reach you, what glory touch you?
Hail, God's mother, delight of the angels;
hail, full of grace, foretold by the prophets' preaching.
The Lord is with you.
The child you bore has saved the world.

Anon, Sixth century

Sleep, holy Babe, upon thy mother's breast;
Great Lord of earth and sea and sky,
How sweet it is to see thee lie
In such a place of rest.

Sleep, holy Babe. Thine angels watch around,
All bending low with folded wings,
Before the Incarnate King of kings,
In reverent awe profound.

Sleep, holy Babe, while I with Mary gaze
In joy upon that face a while,
Upon the loving infant smile
Which there divinely plays.

Sleep, holy Babe. Ah, take thy brief repose;
Too quickly will thy slumbers break,
And thou to lengthened pains awake,
That death alone shall close.

E. Caswall

Father of our Lord Jesus Christ,
our glory is to stand before the world
as your own sons and daughters.
May the simple beauty of Jesus' birth
summon us always to love what is most deeply
    human,
and to see your Word made flesh
reflected in those whose lives we touch.

Roman Missal

Sunday after Christmas

The Holy Family

The feast of the Holy Family is a relatively recent one in the Church's year. It was instituted after the First World War to emphasize the importance of the family unit, which had suffered greatly as a result of political upheavals. To begin with this feast followed that of the Epiphany, but now it falls on the Sunday after Christmas, placing it firmly within the Christmas cycle.

Perhaps even more than in the past the family is a threatened institution, yet it is the basic living cell of society. By emphasizing that Jesus lived as a member of an ordinary family we are brought to focus on the relational element of his upbringing. Jesus grew up in a two-parent family which included St Joseph, his foster father. He was inserted too into an extended family of cousins, aunts, grandparents and neighbours. A full circle of love surrounded him in his growing years. He knew the blessings of a home where mother and father supported one another in sorrow and shared their common joys.

The crib scene is not complete without the presence of Joseph. In some way this is *his* special Christmas feast. Joseph completes the picture, he makes Mary and Jesus members of a trio, a family, and not just a duo.

Parents are called to live for one another and for their children. Joseph allows himself to be identified through his relationship with Mary and Jesus. His hope for the future lies in the Son he has been chosen to care for, not in children of his own flesh. He shares with Mary the experience of Bethlehem, of Egypt, and of the years at Nazareth.

We can sometimes forget that Joseph and Mary had to live very closely together. They had to practise the virtues with one another – kindness, compassion, forgiveness. They had to bear with one another's weaknesses, forgive when there was misunderstanding or hurt, be gentle, humble, kind – not just from time to time but every day, so that they grew together as a married couple and did not just remain as two individuals sharing a house but actually pursuing independent paths.

While we speak sometimes of the 'hidden life' of Jesus at Nazareth, that life was only 'hidden' in that, at this point of time, he was not engaged in a ministry of preaching or teaching. He was living as one of a village community, learning a trade, having to relate to those around him in school and daily work, showing respect and obedience to his parents. He was not secluded in some 'religious' setting like that of the Essenes in their monastery by the Dead Sea, nor did he frequent the temple in his youth, apart from the usual pilgrimages of any observant Jew.

That is why many have found in the thought of Nazareth a focus for their own devotion, a meaning for their own life as it traversed the path of 'ordinariness', dailyness, without particular excitement or religious ecstasy. In Nazareth we see the Son of God accepting all that it means to be part of an ordinary family, living an ordinary daily routine, without any special favours or exceptions.

So much of our life can be wasted just in longing to be 'special', to receive some exceptional treatment or honour or recognition. In the Holy Family we see where *true* honour lies. It consists in building up a community of right values, mutual commitment. Often, because we find it hard to be one among many, we do not recognize our unique inner giftedness and the contribution we make to life just by being who we are, content to identify with the poor who have little choice of employment, little opportunity to develop their talents.

Only when we wholeheartedly embark upon this path of the ordinary do we appreciate the asceticism it contains. By it we share in some measure in the lot of families who even at this moment are victims of war, famine, homelessness, destitution. It is the poor who can teach us about sharing – not only things, but ourselves.

At Nazareth people saw just one family like many others, immersed in the common life of the village. Yet the inner reality was that God was growing up as a boy with human parents, preparing to redeem the world. Outwardly, there was absolutely nothing to remark on. Later, these same villagers could not believe that the local carpenter's son was anyone special.

We should pray for the ability to see beneath the surface familiarity we take for granted to the giftedness of each person (including ourselves). There is so much more to life than meets the eye. We are influencing one another on many levels of which we are unaware.

He was made like us in all things that he might be merciful is the Responsary of today's Vespers. These words are very mysterious. It is only when we really embrace the common life and common lot that we receive a glimmer of understanding. Only when we have faced the hardships of just 'being ordinary' can we be merciful to others in their weakness, and in their struggle to accept the pain of being limited and human. In this, Nazareth can become the focus of our contemplation and of our prayer.

* * *

A wife's charm delights her husband,
and her skill puts flesh on his bones.
A silent wife is a gift from the Lord,
and nothing is so precious as her self-discipline.
A modest wife adds charm to charm,
and no scales can weigh the value of her chastity.
Like the sun rising in the heights of the Lord,
so is the beauty of a good wife in her well-ordered
*   home.*
Like the shining lamp on the holy lampstand,
so is a beautiful face on a stately figure.

Sirach 26:13–17

As God's chosen ones, holy and beloved, clothe yourselves
with compassion, kindness, humility, meekness and
patience. Bear with one another and, if anyone has a com-
plaint against another, forgive each other; just as the Lord
has forgiven you, so you also must forgive. Above all,
clothe yourselves with love, which binds everything
together in perfect harmony.

Colossians 3:12–14

Then he went down with them and came to Nazareth, and
was obedient to them. His mother treasured all these things
in her heart.

And Jesus increased in wisdom and in years, and in
divine and human favour.

Luke 2:51–52

While Miriam was away at the well, Joseph prepared the
boy for his matins prayers, for it was the father's sacred

obligation to accustom his sons from earliest childhood to their duties before God, to study Scripture with them and teach them the recitation of the 'Hear, O Israel'. Joseph helped Yeshua to dress and purify his body for the sacred hour before saying the prayer in unison with him.

Later, when Yeshua had grown somewhat older, Joseph would include verses from the Prophets or the Psalms in these morning sessions; or he would run through the Ten Commandments, inscribed separately on one of the parchment scrolls which were widely disseminated among Jews for the education of children. It was the reader of the synagogue who made these scrolls available to parents, and sometimes pious men engaged a scribe to write the Decalogue on pieces of parchment for free distribution among the children of the poor.

Then he sallied out with Yeshua at his side to fill the sheep's manger with fodder in readiness for Miriam's return. He wished the child to learn that man must feed his animals before sitting down to his morning meal. When Miriam came home, Joseph helped her unload the replenished skins of water, filled the troughs from which the animals drank, and poured the remainder into the large earthen pitcher that stood in the doorway of the house for the family's use.

After the washing of their hands Joseph and Yeshua sat down to their first meal of the day. Miriam served hard-baked wheaten loaves, garnished with fresh vegetables – such as onions, radishes and cucumbers when these were in season – and a small charger of olives and dates. Joseph liked to drink down his meal with fresh water or a cup of home-made beer brewed from pearl barley. For Yeshua there was always a bowl of honey milk and a slice of fig cake, dried on the open roof under the sun.

Next Miriam would take a bowl of whey and the rest of the loaves, which she spread on a low stool by her mother's bed where, finally, she seated herself on a bamboo mat to eat her breakfast with old Hannah . . .

After breakfast Miriam changed her mother's couch, made up the other beds, put the dishes away, and swept and dusted the room. And only then did her working day begin in earnest.

Sholem Asch

The gospel tells us that after having been found in the temple, Jesus went down to Nazareth with his Mother and St Joseph and there he remained until the age of thirty years . . . 'and he was subject to them'.

Thus out of a life of thirty-three years, he who is Eternal Wisdom chose to pass thirty of these years in silence and obscurity, submission and labour.

In the sight of his contemporaries the life of Jesus Christ at Nazareth appeared like the ordinary existence of a simple artisan. We see how true this is. Later, when Christ reveals himself in his public life, the Jews of his country are so astonished at his wisdom and his words, at the greatness of his doctrine and the sublimity of his works, that they ask each other: 'How came this man by this wisdom and miracles? Is not this the carpenter's son? Is not his mother called Mary?'

Souls living the inner life and enlightened from on high, love to contemplate the life of Jesus at Nazareth. They find in it a special charm and, moreover, abundant graces of holiness.

Dom Marmion

The Holy Family

Of her flesh he took flesh:
He does take, fresh and fresh,
Though much the mystery how,
Not flesh but spirit now,
And makes, O marvellous!
New Nazareths in us,
Where she shall yet conceive
Him, morning, noon, and eve;
New Bethlems, and he born
There, evening, noon, and morn.
Bethlem or Nazareth,
Men here may draw like breath
More Christ, and baffle death.

                    Gerard Manley Hopkins

The gospel teaches me that, growing in wisdom
Jesus was obedient to Mary and Joseph;
And my heart shows me with what tenderness
He always obeyed his beloved parents.
Now I understand the mystery of the Temple,
The reply, the tone of my lovable King;
Mother, this gentle Child wants you to be the
    example
Of the soul who searches for him in the night of faith.

Since the King of Heaven has willed that his Mother
Be subject to this night, this anguish of heart,
Then is it a good thing to suffer on this earth?
Yes . . . to suffer, when we love, that is purest
    happiness!
Jesus can take back all he has given me,
Tell him he does not need to ask me first;

I know he can hide himself well; but I will wait for
  him
Until the day without sunset when my faith will turn
  to sight.

I know that at Nazareth, Virgin full of grace,
You lived very poorly without asking for anything
  more.
Neither ecstasies, nor miracles, nor other
  extraordinary deeds
Enhanced your life, O Queen of the elect.
The number of the lowly, the 'little ones', is very great
  on earth.
They can raise their eyes to you without any fear.
You are the incomparable Mother
Who walks with them along the common way
To guide them to heaven.

St Thérèse of Lisieux,
translated by Fenella Matthew

Father in heaven, creator of all,
you ordered the earth to bring forth life
and crowned its goodness by creating the human
  family.
In history's moment when all was ready,
you sent your Son to dwell in time,
obedient to the laws of life in our world.
Teach us the sanctity of human love,
show us the value of family life,
and help us to live in peace with all.

Roman Missal

The Holy Family

Let us adore the Son of the living God, who became son in a human family. Lord Jesus, bless our families.

By your obedience to Mary and Joseph, teach us how to respect proper authority and order.

By the love that filled your home, give our families the grace of loving harmony and peace.

Your first intent was the honour of your Father, may God be the heart of all our family life.

Your parents found you teaching in your Father's house, help us, like you, to seek first the Father's will.

By your reunion with Mary and Joseph in the joy of heaven, welcome our dead into the family of the saints.

Roman Breviary

January 1

Mary, the Mother of God

The Motherhood of Mary, the circumcision and naming of Jesus, are all commemorated on this, the eighth day after Christmas. Jesus, the Redeemer, sheds the first drops of his blood when held in the arms of his mother. As a priest Mary offers the Father his only begotten Son, while his flesh is marked with the sign of the Covenant made with Abraham at the very beginning of Israel's history. The infant also receives his given name of Jesus, which means Saviour. It is the same name as that of Joshua who led the chosen people into the Promised Land after the Exodus from Egypt.

Mary as Mother glories now in the bodiliness of her child, his formal entry into the Israelite community of faith, and his being given the name that will be his for eternity.

The Church also puts Mary before us as the one who meets us at the gate of a new calendar year. It is as though all Christians were being reminded that Mary can most simply and effectively teach us how to follow her Son in the year just beginning.

Looking at Mary we understand, even if only 'as in a mirror darkly', what it means to be a Christ-bearer – a channel of life and love for others.

When we see her with her Child in her arms, or meeting Joseph's gaze, or busying herself with her daily tasks, we see a woman wholly at home in her body, as a woman is when she has experienced the elemental act of giving birth. Yet this feast reminds us too that Mary is the Mother of God, not just mother of the infant Jesus. She transcends the merely physical in her role as God-bearer. She enshrines in her flesh the fulfilment of a mother with the wholeness and integrity of virginity.

René Voillaume says that in the spiritual life it is well nigh impossible to persevere beyond the first stages unless we receive either the gift of contemplation or the gift of deep tenderness for others. Either of these gifts will take us beyond ourselves, and the choice is not ours but God's.

But why should we not, whatever our natural bent, ask for both of these gifts? – for in Mary we see both lived to perfection. She is a woman of prayer, pondering God's words and deeds in silent wonder; but she is also, by her very vocation to motherhood, concerned with practical service, with *expressed* tenderness, with outgoing love, care and concern.

Mary reminds the Church that every child needs a mother, even when that child is the Son of God. Without her body being made available Jesus would not have been born. Without her attending to his bodily needs he could not have grown to maturity. Without her care he would have been emotionally and physically stunted.

Whatever our own physical state, we are called to carry and bear the Lord as Mary did. There is no better resolution for the New Year. And there is no better practice of prayer than to allow the Holy Name of Jesus, which he received this day, to descend into our hearts and become one with our breathing, that we may share his Spirit as a true child of the Eternal Father.

Mary,
May I too long to bear him
for those who are barren, alone;
awaiting they know not what,
or whom,
hearts black as ebony,
heavy as stone.

Let me not rush the gestation,
give Birthling full time to mature.
Humbly, with energy,
serve in the waiting.
Know how to endure.

In the end, warmth and new life
will emerge to the light,
mysteriously formed from my flesh
in the darkness of night.

* * *

*The Lord himself will give you a sign. Look, the young
woman is with child and shall bear a son, and shall name
him Immanuel (God-with-us).*

Isaiah 7:14

*'See, I am bringing good news of great joy for all people:
to you is born this day in the city of David a Saviour, who
is the Messiah, the Lord. This will be a sign for you: you
will find a child wrapped in bands of cloth and lying in a
manger.' And suddenly there was with the angel a multitude of the heavenly host, praising God and saying,*

*'Glory to God in the highest heaven, and on earth peace
among those whom he favours!'*

Luke 2:10–14

*After eight days had passed, it was time to circumcise the
child; and he was called Jesus, the name given by the angel
before he was conceived in the womb.*

Luke 2:21

By your miraculous birth of the Virgin you have fulfilled
the Scriptures: like a gentle rain falling upon the earth you
have come down to save your people. O God we praise
you.

Vespers antiphon, 1 January

In the revised ordering of the Christian period it seems to
us that the attention of all should be directed towards the
restored Solemnity of Mary the holy Mother of God. This
celebration, placed on 1 January in conformity with the
ancient indication of the liturgy of the City of Rome, is
meant to commemorate the part played by Mary in the
mystery of salvation. It is meant also to exalt the singular
dignity which this mystery brings to the 'holy Mother ...
through whom we were found worthy to receive the
Author of Life'. It is likewise a fitting occasion for renewing
adoration of the new-born Prince of Peace, for listening
once more to the glad tidings of the angels, and for implor-
ing from God, through the Queen of Peace, the supreme
gift of peace.

Pope Paul VI

Father,
source of light in every age,
the Virgin conceived and bore your Son
who is called Wonderful God, Prince of Peace.

May her prayer, the gift of a mother's love,
be your people's joy through all ages.
May her response, born of a humble heart,
draw your spirit to rest on your people.

Roman Missal

St Gertrude relates that hearing one day, in the chanting of
the Divine Office, those words of the Gospel naming Christ
'The Firstborn Son of the Virgin Mary', she said to herself:
'The title of Only Son would seem to be more fitting for Jesus
than that of First-born.' While she was dwelling on this
thought, Mary appeared to her: 'No,' said she, 'it is not
"Only Son" but "First-born Son" which is most befitting;
for after Jesus, my sweetest Son, or more truly, in him and
by him, I have given birth to you all in my heart and you
have become my children, the brothers and sisters of Jesus.'

All Christian life consists in forming Christ within us
and making him live in us. This is the idea of St Paul. Now
where was Christ first formed? In the Virgin's womb, by the
operation of the Holy Spirit. But Mary bore Jesus first by
faith and love, when by her *Fiat* she gave the awaited consent. Let us ask her to obtain for us this faith that will make
Jesus dwell in us, this love which will make us live by the life
of Jesus. Let us ask her that we may become like to her Son.
There is no greater favour we can ask her; neither is there
one she wishes more to grant us. For she knows, she sees,
that her Son cannot be separated from his Mystical Body;
she remains so united in heart and soul to her divine Son
that, now in glory, she only desires one thing, and this is that
the Church, the kingdom of the elect, bought with the Blood
of Jesus, should appear before him as a 'glorious Church not
having spot or wrinkle, but holy and without blemish.'

Dom Marmion

Listen, daughter, and behold:
you have become a daughter of your Son,
handmaiden of your Child,
mother of your Creator,
bearer of the most high Redeemer.
The King has fallen in love
with the splendour of your beauty
and has deigned to prepare for himself
a most pure dwelling in his world.
Obtain for us, therefore, from him
who, taken by longing for you, made you his mother,
to pour into us the wondrous sweetness of desire for
    him,
so that we remain dedicated to his service in this life,
and our journey o'er, without chaos, we arrive
with him who was born of you.

Visigothic Book of Prayer,
Seventh century

Hail, O torrent of compassion,
river of peace and of grace,
splendour of purity, dew of the valleys:
Mother of God and mother of forgiveness.
Hail, only salvation of your children,
solemn throne of majesty,
place of shelter, temple of Christ,
the way to life, lily of chastity.
Hail, spouse of Christ,
flower of lovable grace,
humble maidservant.
Most beautiful and worthy of reverence,
no other woman was or can be like you.
We acclaim you, revered one,

your spirit is pure, your heart simple, your body
 chaste.
You are indulgent and merciful,
dear to God, beloved above all.
The person who savours you, ardently desires you
 still,
still thirsts for your holy sweetness,
and always unfulfilled, confines the longing
to loving you and praising you.

Ildefonsus of Toledo, 667

O God, who in the fullness of time
have revealed the splendour of your radiant being
through the motherhood of the Holy Virgin,
so that, to dispel the shadows of sin
truth shines with endless light.
Give us, we pray, the power to adore for ever,
with faith intact and humble demeanour,
the mystery of such an Incarnation,
and to exalt it with true adoration.

Scroll of Ravenna

Blessed are you, O Mary, daughter of the poor,
who became Mother of the Lord of kings.
In your womb he has dwelt
of whose praise the heavens are full.
Blessed be your breast, which has nourished him with
 love,
your mouth which has lulled him
and your arms which have held him.
You have become a vehicle to bear a God of fire!

Blessed are you, O Mary, you have become the home
of the king.
In you, he who has power has taken abode,
he who rules the world.
You came from the tribe of Judah;
you descended from the family of David.
Illustrious is your lineage.
For you, though remaining virgin,
have become the mother of the Son of David.

Blessed are you, O maiden,
who have borne the lion cub spoken of by Jacob . . .
He humbled himself . . . and became a lamb,
destined to ascend the Cross to deliver us.
He prefigured you, the tree,
which, providing the kid, spared the life of Isaac.

Blessed are you, O blessed, since through you
the curse of Eve has been destroyed . . .
From you has come the light
which has destroyed the reign of darkness.

Ephrem the Syrian, 373

January 6

The Epiphany

The Epiphany is celebrated not primarily as an event but as an inner reality. Christ appears among us and reveals his glory.

On Christmas Day we stand around the manger to remember an historical happening. The human setting is uppermost in our minds. At the Epiphany we proclaim that this is no ordinary Child. He comes among us as God, 'manifests' himself to those who choose to see beyond appearances.

That Jesus became a human being requires no proof, he merely had to be born. He is an historical fact whether one is a believer or an atheist. But that this man, this helpless child is God – *that* demands the light of faith, *that* compels adoration.

The manifestation of the Divinity of Christ is commemorated today under three chosen symbols: the adoration of the Magi, showing that he is Saviour and light of the Gentiles who are summoned to adore him; the Baptism in the Jordan, where the Father proclaims him as Son and Beloved; and the wedding at Cana, where Christ as Bridegroom comes to claim his bride, our humanity, changing the water of our natural life into the wine of rejoicing and fulfilment; inviting us, in our turn, to share his divinity.

Today we celebrate the *meaning* of Christmas: that the Word became flesh and dwelt among us, and we saw his glory, glory as of the only Son of the Father full of grace and truth.

Practically speaking we focus today on the Adoration of the Magi. With them we are on a journey, going to find God, and offering him all we have and are, all that is most precious. The Magi's story is our story in that we are part of the gentile world, the world of darkness, the world without God until the advent of the Saviour. The Epiphany celebrates our call to grace and to faith.

The Epiphany, then, is a feast of gift-giving, and in the Eastern Church it is the day when presents are exchanged. We see the Magi travelling many miles to the new-born infant to offer him precious treasure. Then they depart. Such a long way to travel, such a short time in Bethlehem.

It is worth pondering for a few moments on the significance of gifts as we too approach the Child and his Mother. Gifts bind us together in the human community. The Wise Men do not come just to stand and stare. Gifts signify an interchange of relationships, a love and respect for others, a desire to please and honour them with something of our own selves and substance.

Gifts bind us together too because sometimes it is our turn to receive, allowing others the joy of giving us pleasure.

Of course, gifts do not need to be material objects. There are other even more precious things: love, time, friendship, maybe the gift of just being present, adding our voice, our hands, our heart, to the common endeavour. But usually these intangible gifts are exteriorized in some way – a token that bespeaks the reality behind them: a ring, a few flowers, a kiss, a card.

Above all, a gift symbolizes the giving and receiving of love. How unhappy is the child who receives nothing at

Christmas, not an orange, not a hug, not a special smile. That child experiences itself as unloved, even if the words are not said.

But gifts can be misused: they can make others feel small, obligated to return a favour, manipulated. And that is where we can learn from the Wise Men, who proved to be truly wise.

They give their gold, frankincense and myrrh without strings attached. There are no conditions regarding their use, no demanding of time and attention after a long journey. They give with total freedom and disinterestedness.

That is how *we* should give, and that is how *God* loves us in giving us his Son. But God also gives us grace, talents, freedom, invitations to respond to love, so that we have the joy of giving to God in our turn.

What we do with the gifts God gives us is our choice, our responsibility. For each it will be different, and each can give much or little or not at all.

It may be a long hard journey to Bethlehem for us, as it was for the Wise Men, but we can be sure it is worth all the travelling, all the time, all the effort, to glimpse the Child at the end of the journey, and lay our gifts before him in a moment of joy.

* * *

Arise, shine; for your light has come,
and the glory of the Lord has risen upon you.
For darkness shall cover the earth,
and thick darkness the people;
but the Lord will arise upon you,
and his glory appear over you.
Nations shall come to your light,
and kings to the brightness of your dawn.
A multitude of camels shall cover you,

the young camels of Midian and Ephah;
all those from Sheba shall come.
They shall bring gold and frankincense,
and shall proclaim the praise of the Lord.

Isaiah 60:1–3,6

On entering the house, they saw the child with Mary his
mother; and they knelt down and paid him homage. Then,
opening their treasure chests, they offered him gifts of gold,
frankincense, and myrrh.

Matthew 2:11

For there is no distinction between Jew and Greek; the
same Lord is Lord of all and is generous to all who call
upon him. For 'Everyone who calls on the name of the
Lord shall be saved.' But how are they to call on one in
whom they have not believed? And how are they to believe
in one of whom they have never heard? And how are they
to hear without someone to proclaim him? And how are
they to proclaim him unless they are sent? As it is written
'How beautiful are the feet of those who bring good news!'

Romans 10:12–15

At the Epiphany there was a star in the sky, a star on earth
and the Sun in the manger. The star in the sky was the
bright heavenly body; the star on earth, the Virgin Mary;
the Sun in the manger, Christ our Lord.

A star has four main characteristics: it has the nature of
fire, it is bright and clear, it sends forth a ray and it shines
in the night. We can find all these qualities in our star, the
Virgin Mary. She is that burning bush in which the Lord
appeared to Moses, which burned with fire and yet was

not consumed; for though she was with child she was not consumed by the flames of desire. She is in herself bright and splendid, so that it was said of her in the Song of Songs: 'Who is she that cometh forth as the morning rising, fair as the moon, clear as the sun?' And she has sent forth from herself a ray which pierces to the secret places of the heart, and searches the heart and reins; this is the living Word of God, quick and powerful, and sharper than any two-edged sword, piercing even to the dividing asunder of soul and spirit. The meaning of her name is very fitting, for Mary means 'star of the sea'. For she shines on the world like an incomparable star, and her brightness makes the world light, and she has sent forth from herself that ray 'which enlightens everyone who comes into the world' . . . Such is our star, such is the Virgin Mary, the star of the sea, and because she has left us an example, that we should follow her steps, of such kind should our souls be.

St Peter Damien, 1072

The Magi at Bethlehem represent the Gentiles in their vocation to the light of the gospel. The way in which the Magi acted shows us the qualities that our faith ought to have. What is at first apparent is the generous fidelity of this faith . . . and they are our models, whether it concerns the vocation to faith or whether it be a question of the call to perfection.

There is indeed for every faithful soul a vocation to holiness: 'Be holy for I am holy.' The manifestation of this vocation is for each of us his or her star. It takes different forms according to God's designs, our character, the circumstances wherein we live, the events that befall us; but it shines in the soul of each one.

And what is the end and object of this call? For us as for the Magi, it is to lead us to Jesus. The Heavenly Father causes the star to shine in us; for Christ himself says 'No one can come to me except those drawn to me by the Father.'

If with fidelity we listen to the divine call, if we generously press onwards with our gaze fixed upon the star, we shall come to Christ who is the life of our souls. And whatever be our sins, our failings, our miseries, Jesus will welcome us . . .

The heavenly Father calls us to his Son by the inspirations of grace. Like the Magi, as soon as the star shines in our hearts, we should instantly leave all: our sins, the occasions of sin, evil habits, infidelities, imperfections. Taking no account of criticism, nor human opinion, nor the difficulties of the work to be done, we should set out at once to seek Jesus.

Lord, I have seen your star and I come to you. What would you have me do?

Dom Marmion

The incident of the Magi teaches us that hardship, anxiety, pain and harsh circumstances must always prepare the way for the discovery of the Child in its mother's arms. We do not find the herald of God or God himself in easy circumstances. The Child of Mary, many years later, warned his hearers of this, saying: 'But what went you out to see? A man clothed in soft garments? Behold, those clothed in soft garments are in the houses of kings.'

Edward Leen

They leave the land of gems and gold,
The shining portals of the East;
For him, the Woman's seed foretold,
They leave the revel and the feast.

To earth their sceptres they have cast,
And crowns by kings ancestral worn;
They track the lonely Syrian waste;
They kneel before the Babe new-born.

O happy eyes that saw him first;
O happy lips that kissed his feet;
Earth slakes at last its ancient thirst;
With Eden's joy her pulses beat.

He, he is King, and he is alone,
Who lifts that infant hand to bless;
Who makes his mother's knee his throne,
Yet rules the starry wilderness.

Aubrey de Vere

The Virgin herself, the star of the sea, offered these same gifts in her own person to the Sun who was born of her. She offered the gold of royal majesty, for she herself was of kingly race. She offered frankincense and myrrh too, and so we read of her in the Song of Songs: 'Who is this that cometh out of the wilderness like pillars of smoke, perfumed with myrrh and frankincense, with all the powders of the merchant?' Myrrh guards the bodies of the dead from worms and preserves them from corruption; this is why Nicodemus brought a mixture of myrrh and aloes to embalm the body of Jesus. Myrrh symbolizes the purity of the flesh, and frankincense the devotion of spirit. We do well to perceive these qualities in our virgin star,

for purity of body and devotion of spirit alike endured for
ever in the Virgin Mary. And it is right that 'all the powders
of the merchant' should be added; for she deserved to hear
the greeting: 'Hail, full of grace, the Lord is with thee,
blessed art thou among women and blessed is the fruit of
thy womb.' These are the gifts which were offered by the
wise men and by the Virgin Mary. And since they have
given us an example, let us do likewise.

St Peter Damien

Mary, purest flower of earth,
Mary, gate of heaven,
Mary, who to nature's dearth
Mercy's fount hast given;
Mary, Queen of virtues rarest,
Mary, who salvation barest,
Mary, house with treasures stored,
Lead me to my King adored.

Traditional

What shall we present unto thee, O Christ,
For thy coming to earth for us?
Each of thy creatures brings thee a thank-offering:
The angels – singing; the heavens – a star;
The wise men – treasures; the shepherds – devotion;
The earth – a cave; the desert – a manger;
But we offer thee the virgin mother.
O eternal God, have mercy upon us.

Orthodox liturgy

She looked to east, she looked to west,
her eyes unfathomable, mild,
They saw both worlds, came home to rest –
Home to her own sweet child.
God's golden head was on her breast.

What need to look o'er land and sea?
What could the winged ships bring to her?
What gold or gems of price might be,
Ivory or miniver,
Since God himself lay on her knee?

What could th'intense blue heaven keep
To draw her eyes and thoughts so high?
All heaven was where her Boy did leap,
Where her foot quietly
Went rocking the dear God to sleep.

The angel folk fared up and down
A Jacob's ladder hung between
Her quiet chamber and God's Town,
She saw unawed, serene;
Since God himself played by her gown.

Katherine Tynan

February 2

The Presentation in the Temple

'What does the Lord God ask of you except to act justly, to love tenderly and to walk humbly with your God' (cf., Micah 6:8). In the people we meet on the feast of the Presentation these qualities are in evidence throughout: justice, tenderness, humility, as the child Jesus comes to his Father's house for the first time.

Simeon, Anna, Mary, Joseph form a radiant ambience around the child, to welcome and cherish him. This celebration concludes the Christmas cycle which began with Advent, moved through Christmas and Epiphany, and culminates in this feast of light.

St Luke in his Gospel has actually conflated two separate events into one. Firstly, there is the purification of the mother who, after childbirth, is permitted to rest and enjoy her baby before partaking once more in public life and worship. The second is the redemption of the first-born, for every male child who was the eldest son was supposed to belong to God in a special way in memory of the slaying of the Egyptian first-born at the time of the Exodus. Every first-born male animal was offered in sacrifice to symbolize God's dominion over and gift of life; but as a child could not be sacrificed in this way an animal was substituted. In the event of the family being too poor to afford a lamb, then two turtle doves or two young pigeons were acceptable.

Mary and Joseph bring with them the offering of the poor as they make their way through the great colonnades of the Court of the Gentiles towards the Court of the Women. They are hidden in the press of other parents on the same mission, each couple proudly carrying an infant, many of whom would be far more richly arrayed and attended than the swaddled Jesus.

But the aged Simeon recognizes the promised Messiah and takes the Child in his arms. Simeon is an icon of the heavenly Father who accepts this offering of his Son, an offering which will be consummated on the Cross. From being placed in Simeon's arms, Jesus commends himself at the end into the hands of his heavenly Father as he breathes his last.

And Mary hears something more than she heard from the angel Gabriel at the Annunciation when her Son was named as heir to the Davidic Kingdom. Now she hears he is to be a Light to the Gentiles, the glory of Israel, but also a dividing sword, a Child destined to cause his Mother much anguish.

In this feast the light of Christ heralded at Advent comes full circle and points towards Easter. We shall not hold candles again until the Mass of the Easter Vigil when Christ is risen indeed, and the glory he brings can never be extinguished.

To receive a candle into our hands is a symbol of receiving Christ. A candle is given to us at Baptism as a sign that Christ is to be our light and companion through life. Every day, every minute, Mary is placing Jesus in our arms so that we may recognize and cherish him, and yet so often our attention is elsewhere and we miss his presence. We are like the crowds in the temple during Jesus' Presentation. Like them we see just an anonymous infant, one among many, and we take no further notice. We do not recognize God in human guise.

Among all the worshippers only Simeon and Anna had a glimpse into the real nature of the Child in Mary's arms and welcomed him with love. The end of a long life of fidelity was rewarded with true insight. The Spirit revealed to them who the Child really was. They could not have obtained or merited this by themselves.

However, Simeon and Anna had done what they could. Like Mary and Joseph they had acted justly, loved tenderly, walked humbly with God, and so the Spirit was able to take them further. They recognized the Lord and could depart in peace, rejoicing.

The Presentation is a beautiful, lyrical feast; a feast of the temple, of Mary as light-bearer, of Jesus as Lord. The liturgy is uplifting and poetic. But this is all on the exterior level. We have to enter into the reality, take the child Jesus into our own arms, open our hearts, like Mary, ready for the Word of the Lord to pierce us, showing us our weakness and sinfulness, our need of a Saviour. Only when we recognize this need and try to be faithful can the Spirit reveal all he wants to give us.

A Child lies sleeping in darkest night,
Radiant and soft in the candlelight.

He is the One who is Israel's glory,
The Gentile's God in the Temple story.

Joyfully let us acclaim him, beholding
The Mother the Son of the Father enfolding.

But the silent Word once in Temple shown
Is only by silent beholding now known.

And the heart must be pierced by pain and by joy
From the light that flows out from this innocent Boy.

If I hold him close he will break and burn,
But only that I too may glow in my turn.

* * *

The Lord said to Moses: Consecrate to me all the first-born;
whatever is first to open the womb among the Israelites,
of human beings and animals, is mine.

Exodus 13:1

See, I am sending my messenger to prepare the way before
me, and the Lord whom you seek will suddenly come to
his temple. The messenger of the covenant in whom you
delight – indeed he is coming, says the Lord of hosts. But
who can endure the day of his coming, and who can stand
when he appears?
  For he is like a refiner's fire and like fullers' soap; he
will sit as a refiner and purifier of silver, and he will
purify the descendants of Levi and refine them like gold
and silver, until they present offerings to the Lord in righ-
teousness.

Malachi 3:1–3

When the time came for their purification according to the
law of Moses, they brought him up to Jerusalem to present
him to the Lord.
  Guided by the Spirit, Simeon came into the temple; and
when the parents brought in the child Jesus, to do for him
what was customary under the law, Simeon took him in
his arms and praised God, saying:

The Presentation in the Temple

'Master, now you are dismissing your servant in
    peace,
according to your word;
for my eyes have seen your salvation,
which you have prepared in the presence of all
    peoples,
a light for revelation to the Gentiles
and for glory to your people Israel.'

And the child's father and mother were amazed at what
was being said of him. Then Simeon blessed them and said
to his mother Mary, 'This child is destined for the falling
and rising of many in Israel, and to be a sign that will be
opposed so that the inner thoughts of many will be revealed
– and a sword will pierce your own soul too.'

Luke 2:22,27–35

On the feast of the Purification of the Blessed Virgin, early
in the morning, a voice spoke to me saying 'This is the
hour in which Our Lady, the virgin Mary, came with her
Son into the temple.' And my soul heard this with great
love. Then was my soul lifted up, and I saw Our Lady
entering at this hour into the temple, and my soul went to
meet her with great reverence and love. And when for a
little while I was afraid to come close to her, Our Lady
herself gave my soul great security, and held out to me her
Son Jesus and said: 'O lover of my Son, take him!' and she
placed her Son in my arms, and he seemed to me to have his
eyes closed as if he slept, and he was wrapped in swaddling
clothes.

Moreover, Our Lady sat down as if wearied by her journey, and made such beautiful and pleasing signs, and her
presence was so good and gracious, and it was so sweet

and pleasant a thing to see her, that my soul not only regarded the Child Jesus, whom she held so closely in her arms, but was forced also to look upon his mother . . . And the look in the Child's eyes made me feel such love that I was overcome. For from those eyes there went forth so great a splendour and fire of love and joy, that it is unutterable.

Angela of Foligno

See, then, what we shall be if we are to prepare ourselves to be offered in the temple by Mary – faithful, tranquil, simple and trustful; blind as one becomes blind through an excess of light. Then will she carry us in her arms, and each of our actions, offered by her to the Father, will have an infinite value. For a soul thus abandoned there are no longer any little things. To fulfil the most ordinary household duties – everything is so precious when offered at Mary's hands . . .

It is a lovely thing, indeed, to feel oneself abandoned into those pure hands. How sure one is of not straying; what assurance does not their very purity impart. Mary has no need of purification, but we need it, everyone of us, if we are to receive Jesus the Light of the Father.

And finally she lifts us up in her arms and presents us to the Father. He gazes unceasingly at us, and we at him. This 'face to face' is the highest form of the interior life; it is thus that St Paul describes heaven. We shall no longer see him, he says, in the mirror of creatures, but 'face to face'.

A Carthusian

The Presentation in the Temple

Be glad in heart, grow great before the Lord
for thy comfort, and build up glory;
hold thy hoard locked, bind fast thy thought
in thine own mind. Many a thing is unknown.
True comrades sometimes fall away, tired,
word-promises grow faint; so fares this world,
going swiftly in showers, shaping its destiny.
There is one faith, one living Lord,
one Baptism, one Everlasting Father,
one Lord of peoples, who made the world,
its good things and joys. Its glory grew
through this passing earth, stood for a long time
hidden in gloom, under a dark helm,
well screened by trees, overshadowed by darkness,
till a brave-hearted maid grew up among
  mankind.
There it pleased him who shaped all life,
the Holy Spirit, to dwell in her treasure house –
bright on her breast shone the radiant Child
who was the beginning of all light.

Anon, Eighth century

The most chaste Virgin Mother of God bore in her arms
the true light and came to the help of those who were lying
in darkness. In the same way we must hurry out to meet
him who is truly light, enlightened by the beams of his
brightness, and bearing in our hands the light which shines
for all people.

Indeed this is the mystery which we celebrate, that the
light has come into the world and has given its light when
it was shrouded in darkness, and that the dayspring has
visited us from on high and given light to those who were

sitting in darkness. That is why we go in procession with lamps in our hands and hasten bearing lights, showing both that the light has shone upon us, and signifying the glory which is to come to us through him. Therefore let us all run together to meet God.

We have seen God made flesh with our very eyes and we are called the new Israel now that we have seen the visible presence of God and have cradled him in our minds. That presence we celebrate with a yearly festival: we shall never forget it.

St Sophronius, 638

Joy! Joy! The Mother comes, and in her arms she
    brings
The Light of all the world, the Christ, the King of
    Kings;
And in her heart the while all silently she sings.

Saint Joseph follows near, in rapture lost and love,
While angels round about in glowing circles move,
And o'er the Mother broods the Everlasting Dove.

There in the temple court doth Simeon's heart beat
    high,
And Anna feeds her soul with food of prophecy;
But see! The shadows pass, the world's true Light
    draws nigh.

O Infant God, O Christ, O Light most beautiful,
Thou comest Joy of Joys all darkness to annul;
And brightest lights of earth beside thy light are dull.

F. W. Faber

The Presentation in the Temple

Almighty, ever-living God,
on this day your Only-begotten Son
was presented in the temple,
in flesh and blood like ours:
purify us in mind and heart
that we may meet you in your glory.

Roman Breviary

February 11

Our Lady of Lourdes

Four years after the promulgation of the dogma of the Immaculate Conception in 1854, the Blessed Virgin appeared to a fourteen-year-old child, Bernadette Soubirous, whose family were living in poverty in the village of Lourdes in the Pyrenees.

Bernadette was out gathering sticks with her younger sister and a friend when she saw a young girl, clad in pure white, with a sky-blue girdle round her waist, standing in a rocky grotto above the river Gave. A golden rose adorned each foot and she carried a rosary on her arm. The apparition beckoned to Bernadette to say the rosary with her, and with child-like simplicity Bernadette obeyed.

On subsequent occasions Bernadette received a number of messages. There was a call to prayer and penance, the discovery of a spring that proved to have healing qualities, and the request to build a church so that people could come there in procession. Finally, on the feast of the Annunciation the apparition revealed her name, 'I am the Immaculate Conception'.

Since that time Lourdes has been a place of pilgrimage, most especially for the sick and poor. Bernadette's innocence and simplicity, her courageous adherence to the truth of her story in the face of official opposition, her refusal to take money for her very poor family, all eventually convinced the church authorities that she spoke the truth.

Bernadette later joined the Sisters of Charity at Nevers, where she spent the rest of her short life in simple tasks and the care of the infirm sisters. Her health, never robust, soon gave way completely. To the very end she affirmed the reality of what she had seen, and proved it by her own life of service and hidden love. Bernadette is as much the 'miracle of Lourdes' as the vision itself. A very simple person can be used by God for his purposes, as Bernadette allowed herself to be; 'a broom that, when used, can be left behind a door,' as she put it.

Usually the Church does not commemorate particular apparitions; but she has made an exception in the case of Lourdes because of the shrine's popularity in Western Europe, and as an affirmation of the dogma of the Immaculate Conception. Mary, the beautiful woman 'clothed with the sun' does not forget the sufferings of her children on earth.

The feast of Our Lady of Lourdes usually stands on the threshold of Lent and encapsulates many of its themes.

At the opening of the Gospel is the call to repentance; 'Repent and believe the good news.' This is the symbolism of the Lenten ashes and it is echoed at Lourdes, where the Blessed Virgin asks for prayer and penance. Lourdes is a place of repentance in the sense of turning right round, being converted anew, taking one's baptismal promises seriously.

Repentance is to rely on God, not self, to accept that heaven is all around us; the doors are wide open and the Father is waiting if only we turn and look at him. In Bernadette's call to penance there was always a note of freedom and joy, not morbidity. The Father is always ready to welcome us home.

Then the second theme linking Lourdes with Lent is that of forgiveness.

Water symbolizes cleansing and healing. Wounds that

are left unwashed turn septic, wounds that are cleansed and exposed to the air heal naturally. And Lent is a time when we prepare once more to renew baptismal promises and be immersed in the waters of the font, dying and rising with Christ to new life.

Many come to the waters of Lourdes, not just for physical cures but for grace and strength to bear pain. This is the most usual result of a pilgrimage.

We all long for wholeness; for the old wounds and sores of sin to be healed, and for life to flow through us anew. One of the lessons of Lourdes is that it is in giving to others, those who are less fortunate than ourselves, that we come to wholeness. It is by generously reaching out, not by looking at our own sickness, that we discover life and hope once more.

Mary at Lourdes is mother to the sick and the needy, mother to each one who looks to her with confidence. We have to trust that love truly is stronger than all physical or spiritual evil. It is never too late to turn to Mary's Son and repent.

* * *

O my dove, in the clefts of the rock, in the covert of
*   the cliff,*
let me see your face, let me hear your voice;
for your voice is sweet and your face is lovely.

Song of Songs 2:14

Rejoice with Jerusalem and be glad for her,
all you who love her;
rejoice with her in joy, all you who mourn over her –
that you may nurse and be satisfied from her
*   consoling breast;*

that you may drink deeply with delight
from her glorious breasts.
For thus says the Lord:
I will extend prosperity to her like a river,
and the wealth of the nations like an overflowing
    stream;
and you shall nurse and be carried on her arm,
and dandled on her knees.
As a mother comforts her child, so will I comfort you;
you shall be comforted in Jerusalem.

Isaiah 66:10–13

Then I saw a new heaven and a new earth; for the first
heaven and the first earth had passed away, and the sea
was no more. And I saw the holy city, the new Jerusalem,
coming down out of heaven from God, prepared as a bride
adorned for her husband. And the one who was seated on
the throne said, 'See, I am making all things new.' Also he
said, 'Write this, for these words are trustworthy and true.

'To the thirsty I will give water as a gift from the spring
of the water of life. Those who conquer will inherit these
things, and I will be their God and they will be my
children.'

Revelation 21:1–2,5,6b–7

Coming out of the light of the rising sun ... is the Virgin,
the Immaculate Conception ... No wonder that at this
sight wounds are healed, crippled and distorted frames are
set straight, blocked senses are opened up, torn tissues are
renewed, oppressed hearts expand, and poor whole selves,
body and soul, are called to be that image of the image of
God, so splendid, humble, triumphant, grateful, faithful,

prayerful, up yonder. She crushes underfoot the dry thorns of winter, and June roses have already sprung into flower at her feet! She holds out her rosary bidding us to the ascent. Indeed, Mother of God, image of God, it is with thee we would climb rose by rose towards infinite joy . . . And then light dawns for us too and we are ravished and carried away. So it was with the spectators at Lourdes who could not see the Virgin but watched Bernadette's face.

Paul Claudel

How happy my soul was, good Mother, when I had the good fortune to gaze upon you!
How I love to recall the pleasant moments spent under your gaze, so full of kindness and mercy for us.
Yes, tender Mother, you stooped down to earth to appear to a mere child . . .
You, the Queen of heaven and earth deigned, to make use of the most fragile thing in the world's eyes.

St Bernadette

The message of Lourdes is not restricted to the words Bernadette heard in the grotto: prayer and penitence, in the sense of a thoroughgoing conversion of turning towards God. It is to be found, first and foremost, in the poverty embodied in the very choice of Bernadette and in the immediate response of the poor to the good news . . . Finally, the message of Lourdes is ultimately the very name and identity of the messenger, the immaculate Mary, the virgin of the Magnificat, the prototype of the Church and of a radical and total living out of the Gospel.

René Laurentin

The Blessed Virgin's role as Mother leads the people of God to turn with filial confidence to her who is ever ready to listen with a mother's affection and efficacious assistance. Thus the People of God have learned to call upon her as the Consoler of the Afflicted, the Health of the Sick, the Refuge of Sinners, that they may find comfort in tribulation, relief in sickness and liberating strength in guilt. For she, who is free from sin, leads her children to combat sin with energy and resoluteness. This liberation from sin and evil, it must be repeated, is the necessary premise for any renewal of Christian living.

Pope Paul VI

It is a good thing to make a pilgrimage to Lourdes, at least in spirit. The Blessed Virgin has all sorts of things to say to us. Rather, she waits to tell us what we already know, the only saving things, in a way that will lead us to accept and love them better. How much Lourdes resembles the gospel, for anyone willing to open their hearts and listen . . .

How wonderfully Lourdes proclaims the gospel. One cannot but be tempted to compare the simple and clear words of the apparition with the simplicity and clarity of the beginning of St Luke's Gospel – the announcement to Mary, and to the world, of the incarnation.

One cannot go wrong here, for the words are all of the same source and inspiration, of the same Spirit. The one guarantees the other. It is the same heart and soul, the same Mary, who listens to the angel and who speaks to Bernadette. It is the same Spirit who gives Mary the grace to understand the angel's message, and who moves her to speak to Bernadette according to God's will.

The faithful and simple response of Bernadette is a replica of Mary's. An innocent girl, ignorant of evil and wishing to know none, unpretentious and simple, putting herself at God's disposal, strong in humility and, because of her humility, strong and firm in reacting to the divine Word: such was Mary and so was Bernadette to be.

Gabriel Cardinal Garonne

In the shadow of your mercy we shelter,
O holy Mother of God.
Despise not our prayers in our necessity,
but deliver us always from all dangers
O ever-glorious and blessed Virgin Mary.

Anon, Third century

O holy Virgin,
in the midst of your days of glory,
do not forget the sorrows of this earth.
Cast a merciful glance upon those who are suffering,
struggling against difficulties,
with their lips constantly pressed against life's bitter
cup.
Have pity on those who love each other and are
separated.
Have pity on our rebellious hearts.
Have pity on our weak faith.
Have pity on those who love.
Have pity on those who weep, on those who pray, on
those who fear.
Grant hope and peace to all. Amen.

Abbé Perreyve

Lord of mercy,
as we keep the memory of Mary,
the immaculate Mother of God,
who appeared to Bernadette at Lourdes:
grant us through her prayer
strength in our weakness
and grace to rise up from our sins.

Roman Breviary

March 19

St Joseph, Husband of Mary

It is only within the last few hundred years that Joseph has been honoured so greatly in the Church. Yet he belongs with Mary in any book about her, for he was her husband, intimately associated with her in the upbringing of Jesus.

When we look at St Joseph we see a craftsman, husband and father of a family, unobtrusively beside Mary as friend and companion.

Joseph is so silent in the Gospels, so 'ordinary' that it was many years before the Church took notice of him. Only with time did Christians come to appreciate his worth, and devotion to him spread throughout Christendom. In this St Teresa of Avila played a notable role, for she dedicated many of her Carmelite convents to St Joseph, and wherever the Order of Carmel spread devotion to St Joseph followed.

But why is Joseph so special? M. Olier says that while every other saint mirrors some aspect of the life of Christ – his prayer, his compassion, his preaching, his love for the poor and so forth – only Joseph was chosen to mirror the Father. Only this man reflects in a unique way the love of the Eternal Father for his only-begotten Son.

We all know how psychologists have demonstrated that much of our conception of God is drawn from significant adults in our early lives – parents, teachers, priests. We depend upon them when we are young, and their attitudes and behaviour shape our ideas of the Divinity, just as they are the models for our own adult development, whether we like it or not! Some time ago I was speaking to the late Donald Nicholl and he told me that he was once asked what he thought was the essence of masculinity. The question came to him unexpectedly, and without thinking he replied 'utterly dependable tenderness'. On reflection he realized that this definition had been drawn spontaneously from the depths of his unconscious, being communicated to him by his own father – and what a wonderful tribute to his father that was!

When we see Jesus the grown man, when we sense his deep love of God, his manliness, his tenderness, his justice, his compassion, his idea of true religion, then we get a glimpse of what Joseph must have meant in his life.

Judaism was, and is, basically a religion for men when it comes to fulfilling religious duties. Women are honoured as queen in their own home, but because of child-rearing, housekeeping, and domestic work, the obligations of the Law sit lightly on them.

Jesus then would have learned his religion primarily from Joseph, by him been initiated into the heritage of the Law and the prophets, by him introduced to worship in the synagogue, by him instructed in what was involved in growing to maturity.

By spending hours with Joseph in the carpenter's shop Jesus would have learned a craft, and been able to support his mother after Joseph's death.

There in the background of the life of Jesus and Mary we recognize a figure ever steadfast, ever just, ever respect ful, ever sensitive – Joseph. He was a loving husband to Mary his wife, a father and friend to the growing boy and young man Jesus.

Joseph lived only for God, with Mary's love and companionship, each supporting the other in a common love for their child.

And how is Joseph also, as St Teresa says, a master of prayer? In the New Testament, we are told very little about him directly. We know he was a 'just man' in the full Old Testament sense of the word. He was intuitive, he attended to his dreams, not even in sleep was he outside God's ambience. We know too that he put God's directives into practice. It was not a matter of pious thoughts only, these were combined with action. He kept the liturgical feasts, going regularly to synagogue and temple. And he lived daily with Mary and Jesus, as we are asked to do in our turn. In their home the psalms and Scriptures were the food of every-day reflection. With Joseph to teach us, we can find in them ever fresh insights without looking for 'signs and wonders' elsewhere.

* * *

Happy is the husband of a good wife;
the number of his days will be doubled.
A loyal wife brings joy to her husband
and he will complete his years in peace.
A good wife is a great blessing;
she will be granted among the blessings of the man
who fears the Lord.
Whether rich or poor, his heart is content,
and at all times his face is cheerful.

Sirach 26:1–4

Now the birth of Jesus the Messiah took place in this way.
When his mother Mary had been engaged to Joseph, but
before they lived together, she was found to be with child

from the Holy Spirit. Her husband Joseph, being a righteous man and unwilling to expose her publicly to disgrace, planned to dismiss her quietly. But just when he had resolved to do this, an angel of the Lord appeared to him in a dream and said, 'Joseph, son of David, do not be afraid to take Mary as your wife, for the child conceived in her is of the Holy Spirit. She will bear a son, and you are to name him Jesus, for he will save his people from their sins.' When Joseph awoke from sleep, he did as the angel of the Lord commanded him; he took her as his wife, but had no marital relations with her until she had borne a son; and he named him Jesus.

Matthew 1:18–21,24–25

All spoke well of him, and wondered at the gracious words that came from his mouth. They said, 'Is not this Joseph's son?'

Luke 4:22

The suit for a girl's hand had to be made to the bride's father. The bridegroom's father or a friend began the negotiations. If the suit was accepted and the girl gave her consent – supposing she was allowed a voice in the matter at all – they then proceeded to bargain about the purchase price, trousseau and dowry . . .

About a year later the wedding took place, and this was a kind of communal festivity, to which as many guests as possible were invited. The climax of it was the bringing home of the bride . . . A bride of good name and well-to-do family was borne in a litter or on a richly caparisoned camel. The wedding banquet followed, and the festivities might last for seven days, if the bridegroom's resources permitted it. There is never any mention of a religious ceremony in connection with a wedding. In the case of poorer people things would be on a more modest scale. Mary and Joseph were not of the wealthy class, even though, on the other hand, their poverty should not be exaggerated. Joseph as an artisan would certainly earn what was necessary for himself and his family.

We do not know how Mary and Joseph were brought together. If ever it was true that happy marriages are made in heaven, it was certainly so in this case. As God had chosen and prepared the mother of his Only-begotten, he also prepared his foster father, who had so important a part to play in the plan of redemption. The husband and wife, bound together for life, now really began to know one another. There were no disillusionments in this case. As day followed day, they found new excellences and lovable qualities in each other, so that their love grew and deepened. They were one in their love and fidelity to God.

J. Patsch

Our Lady's Espousals

Wife did she live, yet virgin did she die,
Untouched of man, yet mother of a son;
To save herself and child from fatal lie,
To end the web whereof the thread was spun,
In marriage knots to Joseph she was tied,
unwonted works with wonted veils to hide.

God lent his paradise to Joseph's care.
Wherein he was to plant the tree of life;
His Son, of Joseph's child the title bare,
Just cause to make the mother Joseph's wife.

St Joseph, Husband of Mary

O blessed man! betrothed to such a spouse,
More blessed to live with such a child in house!

St Robert Southwell, 1595

I took for my advocate and lord the glorious St Joseph and commended myself earnestly to him; and I found that this my father and lord delivered me both from this trouble and also from other and greater troubles concerning my honour and the loss of my soul, and that he gave me greater blessings than I could ask of him. I do not remember even now that I have ever asked anything of him which he has failed to grant. I am astonished at the great favours which God has bestowed on me through this blessed saint, and at the perils from which he has freed me, both in body and soul. To other saints the Lord seems to have given grace to succour us in some of our necessities but of this glorious saint my experience is that he succours us in them all and that the Lord wishes to teach us that as he himself was subject to him on earth (for, being his guardian and being called his father, he could command him) just so in heaven he still does all he asks. This has also been experienced by other people whom I have advised to commend themselves to him; and even today there are many who have great devotion to him through having newly experienced this truth.

Those who practise prayer should have a special affection for St Joseph always. I do not know how anyone can think of the Queen of Angels, during the time that she suffered so much with the Child Jesus, without giving thanks to St Joseph for the way he helped them. If any cannot find a master to teach them how to pray, let them take this glorious saint as their master and they will not go astray.

St Teresa of Avila

Consider the glorious titles of St Joseph.

His was the title of father of the Son of God, because he was the spouse of Mary, ever Virgin. He was our Lord's father, because Jesus ever yielded to him the obedience of a son. He was our Lord's father, because to him were entrusted, and by him were faithfully fulfilled, the duties of a father, in protecting him, giving him a home, sustaining and rearing him, and providing him with a trade.

J. H. Newman

The assumption that St Joseph died before Our Lord's passion and death can hardly be called into question. If it were not so, would the Saviour have commended his mother to St John's care? And if it is so, should we not picture that foster Son, the child of his heart, there to help him at his passing? Blessed are the merciful, they shall obtain mercy ... Think of the mercy, the charity, the kindness, which the foster-father showed towards the Saviour born into the world a tiny babe. It does not bear thinking that this Son, who was God, did not repay him a hundredfold with similar courtesies, overwhelming St Joseph's soul with blessings on its journey from this world.

When the Saviour was still a child, his foster-father, the great St Joseph, and his Mother, the glorious Virgin, had carried him many times – especially on the journey they made from Judea to Egypt, and back again. Surely, then, as that saintly father drew near the end of his days, he was in turn carried by his Son on the journey from this world to the next, to Abraham's bosom – to be transferred from there to glory on the day of the Ascension.

St Francis de Sales

St Joseph, Husband of Mary

Joseph, your admirable life
Took place in poverty,
But you contemplated the beauty
Of Jesus, and Mary.

The Son of God, in his childhood,
Often happily
Submitted to your authority
And rested on your heart.

Like you, we serve Mary and Jesus
In solitude.
Pleasing them is our only aim.
We desire nothing more.

St Thérèse of Lisieux

O St Joseph, guardian of Jesus, chaste spouse of Mary, you who spent your life in the perfect accomplishment of duty, maintaining with the work of your hands the Holy Family of Nazareth, grant your kind protection to those who, full of trust, turn to you now!

You know their desires, their difficulties, their hopes; they pray to you because they know that in you they find one who understands and protects them. You have also known trials, toil and fatigue; yet in the midst of the material cares of life, your soul, full of the most profound peace, rejoiced with indescribable happiness in the close companionship of the Son of God who was entrusted to your care, and of Mary, his sweet Mother.

May those whom you protect understand that they are not alone in their toil: may they perceive Jesus by their side, receive him with grace and guard him faithfully as you did. And with your prayers, obtain that in every family, in every factory or work room, and wherever a Christian works, everything may be sanctified in charity, patience and justice, and in the search for righteousness, so that the gifts of heavenly love may be showered upon them.

Pope John XXIII

Almighty God,
at the beginnings of our salvation,
when Mary conceived your Son and brought him
   forth into the world,
you placed them under Joseph's watchful care.
May his prayer still help your Church
to be an equally faithful guardian of your mysteries,
and a sign of Christ to humankind.

Roman Breviary

Jesus, Mary and Joseph, I give you my heart and my
   soul;
Jesus, Mary and Joseph, assist me in my last agony;
Jesus, Mary and Joseph, may I breathe forth my soul
   in peace with you.

Traditional

March 25

The Annunciation

'We declare to you . . . what we have heard, what we have seen with our eyes, what we have looked at and touched with our hands' (1 John:1).

We say that our religion is an incarnational religion, one which embraces every aspect of the human person, flesh as well as spirit. And we find its origin here in the Incarnation, source and root of our redemption. Mary's 'Yes' is the beginning of a new era. She is the 'new Eve', the woman who consents to life through obedience to the word and call of God.

The mysteries of our redemption meet in Mary. At the Annunciation she says 'yes' to the Incarnation, on Calvary she consents to the final sacrifice of the Cross. When Christ is risen her initial '*Fiat*' is completed in a joy beyond all words.

During the Middle Ages the year was often deemed to begin with this feast, it was considered so important. Mary, the Mother of God, is the one chosen to bear Jesus for the world. He is the new beginning for all humanity, in him we see what we are called to be, just as Mary is the one who shows the perfect response that is asked of us in our turn. The ringing of the Angelus bell three times daily is a constant reminder of the angel's message and Mary's consent, a reminder in the context of our daily work that the Word became flesh and dwelt among us.

Jesus is bone of Mary's bone, flesh of her flesh. But the link is deeper even than this. Mary is one with Jesus because she is a woman of faith, a woman who lived the faith of Abraham to the full, who became in her person all that Israel was meant to be as bride of the Lord.

> I *will betroth you to me forever.*
> I *will betroth you to me in righteousness and in*
>   *justice,*
> *in steadfast love and in mercy,*
> I *will betroth you to me in faithfulness;*
> *and you shall know the lord.*

> *Hosea 2:19–20; RSV*

In her betrothal Mary says 'Yes' in the name of Israel and 'Yes' for us. She is fully responsive, not merely in a passive way, but actively. In receiving the Word, God does not use her blindly. He seeks her consent to his predetermined plan; she co-operates in the work of salvation.

If we want to know what it means to conceive Jesus within us we only have to look to Mary. It means listening to the invitation of God, at first with surprise that we are chosen, then, like her, opening ourselves to the in-pouring of the Spirit so that the Word may take flesh in our own lives. The angel who brings this message may not be a recognizable heavenly being, but a friend, a colleague, a family member, anyone who calls forth our potential for being a Christ-bearer, just as we may be the messenger who tells this good news to someone else, whether we are conscious of the fact or not.

To be receptive to the Spirit is something we can foster in various ways. Erich Fromm points out that love is a way of life which cannot be partitioned off in an assortment of separate compartments, enabling us to say 'I love this but not that.' Love is embodied in all we do if it is real. When the world is our home and the Spirit dwells in us we do not devour and defile. Rather we know how to wait, to watch, to wonder, to touch people and things with reverence, for 'the Lord is with us' and there is nothing outside the sphere of the holy.

The Word becomes flesh today only if he becomes flesh in *my* life, if I attend to the messengers who come to me through events and circumstances and say my personal *'Fiat'*.

If I am open to God's coming, if I make a home for him within my heart and body, then my life will be rooted and founded in love, wise with Mary's own wisdom and peace.

* * *

Sing aloud, O daughter of Zion; shout, O Israel!
Rejoice and exult with all your heart,
O daughter Jerusalem!
The Lord has taken away the judgements against you,
he has turned away your enemies.
The king of Israel, the Lord is in your midst;
you shall fear disaster no more.
The Lord, your God, is in your midst
a warrior who gives victory;
he will rejoice over you with gladness,
he will renew you in his love.

Zephaniah 3:14–15,17

The angel said to her, 'Do not be afraid, Mary, for you have found favour with God. And now, you will conceive in your womb and bear a son, and you will name him Jesus . . .'

'How can this be, since I am a virgin?'

'The Holy Spirit will come upon you, and the power of the Most High will overshadow you; therefore the child to be born will be called holy; he will be called the Son of God . . .'

'Here I am, the servant of the Lord; let it be with me according to your word.'

Luke 1:30–38 (passim)

When the fullness of time had come, God sent his Son, born of a woman, born under the law, in order to redeem those who were under the law, so that we might receive adoption as children.

Galatians 4:4–5

Go to your inward cell with Our Lady St Mary, where she awaited the angel's message; and here do you also wait the angel's coming, so that you may see him when he comes in, and notice how graciously and courteously he greets this gracious maid. And with your whole soul overcome with awe and praise, cry out as loud as you can when the angel begins his salutation to this blessed maid and mother, and say: 'Hail, Mary, full of grace, the Lord is with you! Blessed are you among women, and blessed is the fruit of your womb, Jesus!' And saying this over and over, think how full and welling was the grace in Mary, for from her all the world borrowed and begged grace when God's Son was made man, full of grace and truth. Then wonder greatly in your heart how this Lord who made heaven and earth out of nothing was enclosed within the womb of a small, gentle maiden, whom God the Father hallowed,

whom God the Son had as his Mother, and whom God
the Holy Spirit filled with grace.

Ah! Sweet, blessed Lady,
With how much grace you were visited,
with what burning fire of love you were inflamed
when you felt in your heart and in your womb
the presence of so great majesty!
For Christ took flesh of your flesh,
and of your clean, maidenly blood he took his blood,
and of your members he made his members
in which dwelt the fullness of the Godhead.
All this he did for you, so that you might love this
   maid and mother,
and her Son, Christ, to whom you are wedded.

St Aelred, 1167

Then he brought Our Lady St Mary to my attention. I saw
her spiritually in bodily likeness, a simple, humble maiden,
young in years and little more than a child, in the form in
which she was when she conceived. God also showed me
something of the wisdom and truth of her soul, and
through this I understood her profound and wondering
reverence that he, her creator, should want to be born of
her, someone so simple and of his own making. This wisdom and truth, this knowledge of her creator's greatness
and her own littleness as creature, made her say to Gabriel
in deep humility: 'Behold me here, God's handmaiden.'
In this vision I understood without doubt that, as far as
worthiness and wholeness are concerned, she is superior
to everything else that God has made; for above her there

is nothing in the created order except Jesus Christ in his humanity, as I see it.

Julian of Norwich

Mary,
ground of all being,
Greetings!

Greetings to you, loving and lovely Mother!
You birthed to earth your Son.
You birthed the Son of God from heaven
by breathing the Spirit of God.

Hildegard of Bingen

Our Lady said yes for the human race. Each one of us must echo that yes for our lives.

We are all asked if we will surrender what we are, our humanity, our flesh and blood to the Holy Spirit and allow Christ to fill the emptiness formed by the particular shape of our life.

The surrender that is asked of us includes complete and absolute trust; it must be like Our Lady's surrender, without condition and without reservation.

What we shall be asked to give is our flesh and blood, our daily life, our thoughts, our service to one another, our affections and loves, our words, our intellect, our waking, working and sleeping, our ordinary human joys and sorrows – to God.

To surrender all that we are, as we are, to the Spirit of Love in order that our lives may bear Christ into the world – that is what we shall be asked.

Our Lady has made this possible. Her *fiat* was for herself

and for us, but if we want God's will to be completed in us as it was in her, we must echo her *fiat*.

Caryll Houselander

O alone of all women, Mother and Virgin,
Mother most happy, Virgin most pure,
now we, impure as we are,
come to you who are all pure.
We hail you, we honour you as best we may
with our humble offerings.
May your Son grant us that, imitating your holy
surrender,
we also, by the grace of the Holy Spirit,
may deserve to spiritually conceive the Lord Jesus
in our inmost soul,
and once conceived, never to lose him. Amen.

Fifteenth-century prayer to Our Lady of Walsingham

Almighty Father of our Lord Jesus Christ,
you have revealed the beauty of your power
by exalting the lowly virgin of Nazareth
and making her the mother of our Saviour.
May the prayers of this woman
bring Jesus to the waiting world,
and fill the void of incompletion
with the presence of her Child.

Roman Missal

Let us be guided by the words of Gabriel,
citizen of heaven, and say:
Hail, full of grace, the Lord is with you!
We say again with him:

Hail, O our much longed-for joy!
Hail, O rapture of the Church!
Hail, O name so full of fragrance!
Hail, O countenance illuminated by the light of God
   from which such beauty flows!
Hail, O memorial full of reverence!
Hail, O spiritual and salutary fleece!
Hail, O bright mother of the dawning light!
Hail, O stainless mother of saintliness!
Hail, O gushing fount of living water!
Hail, new mother, moulder of the new-born One!
Hail, O inexplicable and mystery-filled mother! . . .
Hail, O alabaster vase of holy unction!
Hail, you who give honour to virginity!
Hail, O humble space, which welcomed to itself
Him whom the world cannot contain!

Theodotus of Ancrya,
Fifth century

'Ave Maria'; o'er the earth and sea,
That heavenliest hour of heaven is worthiest thee.

'Ave Maria'; blessed be the hour,
The time, the clime, the spot, where I so oft
Have felt the moment in its fullest power
Sink o'er the earth so beautiful and soft,
While swung the deep bell in the distant tower,
Or the faint dying day-hymn stole aloft,
And not a breath crept through the rosy air,
And yet, the forest leaves seemed stirred with prayer.

'Ave Maria'; 'tis the hour of prayer;
'Ave Maria'; 'tis the hour of love;
'Ave Maria'; may our spirits dare

The Annunciation

Look up to thine and to thy Son's above;
'Ave Maria'; oh, that face so fair;
Those downcast eyes beneath the Almighty Dove –
What though 'tis but a pictured image strike,
That painting is no idol – 'tis too like.

Lord Byron

Mary,
The heavens gift the earth with moist dew.
The entire earth rejoices.
From your womb the seed sprouted forth.
The birds of the air nest in this tree.

Blessed is the fruit of your womb!
Your womb's fruitfulness is food for humankind.
Great is the joy of this delicious banquet!
In you, mild Virgin, is the fullness of all joy.

Hildegard of Bingen

Easter

On Easter Sunday, the first after being elected to the Patri-
archate of Venice, Cardinal Roncalli, later Pope John
XXIII, celebrated Benediction in his cathedral, the interior
glowing with candles to light its mysterious darkness. He
thought the service was over when the choir burst into a
hymn, overpowering the senses with its haunting, oriental
melody. The Cardinal turned to an attendant canon to ask
'What now?' And he was directed to the icon of Mary.
'Let us go, your Eminence, to congratulate Our Lady on
her Son's resurrection.'

An ancient tradition in the Church, though not recorded
in the Gospels, is that Jesus appeared to Mary his mother
as first witness of the resurrection. That may or may not
be true, but it is the first meditation given on the Easter
appearances in the Spiritual Exercises of St Ignatius, and
is worth pondering imaginatively, for whether or not Mary
was a witness to the resurrection she must surely have
believed in the reality of her Son's triumph.

Easter is, as it were, another Christmas for Mary. She not
only bore the Redeemer but saw the redemption accomplished. Mary is now the mother of all of us. Everything that
belonged to the earth and to the flesh at Christmas, becomes
at Easter a spiritual reality, open, boundless, ever-present.
The joy of the Annunciation has come to full flower.

Mary's life may not have been particularly 'happy' in

the secular sense of that word; but at the root of her being there must have been a deep joy at being used by the Father for a unique role in salvation history, no matter what may have been the cost to her. An old invocation addresses her as 'Mary, who kept the faith on Holy Saturday'. When all others had lost faith, she remained faithful. And her faith was rewarded, her trust vindicated.

Mary, like us, had to find herself in letting go, allowing her Son to be primarily the Son of the Father, and accomplish the mission he was sent to bring to fulfilment.

Easter is a feast of forgiveness for us, by which we too make space for the risen Lord – let go of his bodily presence, let go of our sin, and become 'space' for him.

Mary in her sinlessness understands sin in a way we could never do. Because she is immaculate she can measure the Son's perfect love better than can Peter or Magdalen. Her soul was totally transparent, empty, renouncing everything, offering everything, as we are asked to do with Christ's grace.

At Easter we remember that Love has conquered sin and death for ever. For Mary his Mother, no proof was needed, for love breaks all barriers. She must have *known*, needed no special sign for herself alone, no mark of forgiveness or appreciation. At the foot of the Cross she *knew*, as none other, that her Son had already entered into his glory. Rejoice O sorrowful Mother and enter now into joy!

She woke that morning to cold, grey dawn,
Her body bereft, her soul red-torn;

When she glimpsed through the door, standing open
    wide,
his footprints dew-wet on the grassy side.

And her heart soared up, like a lark in spring,
For her Son and the new song he now could sing.

And she knew that all who believed would see
Him coming to meet them in Galilee.

Mary, your joy is true and deep;
Your Son has risen forever from sleep.

* * *

The steadfast love of the Lord never ceases,
his mercies never come to an end;
they are new every morning;
great is your faithfulness.
The Lord is my portion, says my soul,
therefore I will hope in him.

Lamentations 3:22–24

But on the first day of the week, at early dawn, they came
to the tomb, taking the spices that they had prepared. They
found the stone rolled away from the door of the tomb,
but when they went in, they did not find the body. While
they were perplexed about this, suddenly two men in dazz-
ling clothes stood beside them, 'Why do you look for the
living among the dead? He is not here, but has risen.
Remember how he told you, while he was still in Galilee,
that the Son of Man must be handed over to sinners, and
be crucified, and on the third day rise again.' Then they
remembered his words, and returning from the tomb, they
told all this to the eleven and to the rest.

Now it was Mary Magdalene, Joanna, Mary the mother
of James, and the other women who told this to the
apostles.

Luke 24:1–10

Easter

If Christ has not been raised, then our proclamation has been in vain and your faith has been in vain.

1 Corinthians 15:14

The death of the Lord is wrapped in mystery. He suffered a death more grievous than any man can suffer because he was more truly alive than any man. And yet, when he spoke of his death, he also spoke of his Resurrection. 'From that time Jesus began to show his disciples that he must go to Jerusalem and suffer many things from the elders and scribes and chief priests, and be put to death, and on the third day rise again.'

The disciples did not understand his words; their whole manner at his death shows this. But she who must have known the truth was Mary. She had given him his human life; his breath and growth; his every movement had taken place before her eyes and heart for thirty years; she had stood beneath the Cross and she had seen him die; so she knew that his life was of a special kind. When the women and Peter and John spoke of the empty tomb and the words of the angel, she already knew he was risen. She had seen him. And she whose heart had been placed in the tomb with the body of her Son, arose with him in the light of his divine victory.

Paul says in the letter to the Romans that 'our old self' should be 'crucified' and die and be 'buried in Christ.' If this happens, then 'as Christ has arisen from the dead through the glory of the Father, so we also may walk in newness of life.' This dying and entombing of the old self is a constant process within us: through the struggle against evil; through the conquest of self; through every suffering bravely borne; through every sacrifice of love and charity.

But through it is also accomplished the resurrection of the new self. At times, very deep within us, and covered by earthly insufficiency and calamities, we feel the secret spark of this ever-holy and living flame, the 'glory of the children of God'. For the rest, we have to believe.

Romano Guardini

A thousand times glorified are you,
O Virgin Mother of God!
We hymn our praise to you,
for by the Cross of your Son
hell has been overthrown and death humiliated;
we, who were dead, have been revived
and made worthy of life.
We have gained paradise, our principal reward.
Therefore we glorify you, O Christ our God,
the almighty and merciful one.

Anon, Fifth–Sixth centuries

The clouds of night are past away;
Rejoice, Marie, rejoice today; Alleluia, Alleluia.
The offspring of thy virgin womb
Has risen from the virgin tomb; Alleluia, Alleluia,
Alleluia.

Death's arrows keen are snapt in twain;
At Jesu's feet death lieth slain; Alleluia, Alleluia.
Though heaviness endure a night,
Joy cometh with the morning light. Alleluia, Alleluia,
Alleluia.

The cross, whereon our debts were paid,
His kingly sceptre he hath made; Alleluia, Alleluia.
Rejoice, Marie, rejoice today;
The clouds of night are past away. Alleluia, Alleluia,
    Alleluia.

Anon, Twelfth century

Whether Mary saw the risen Lord for the first time with the other women, or whether she was granted a separate appearance, in any case she experienced an unspeakably great joy over the victory of her Son. All the sorrow and trouble of her life were now behind her. Jesus' triumph was her triumph too, Jesus' honour was her honour, with his glory began her exaltation too, with the King of heaven and earth his Mother also became Queen of his everlasting kingdom.

J. Patsch

Queen of heaven rejoice. *Alleluia!*
The Son whom it was your privilege to bear *Alleluia!*
Has risen as he said. *Alleluia!*
Pray to God for us. *Alleluia!*
Rejoice and be glad Virgin Mary, *Alleluia!*
For the Lord has truly risen. *Alleluia!*

Let us pray;
O God you were pleased to give joy to the world through the Resurrection of your Son, our Lord, Jesus Christ. Grant we beseech you that through the intercession of the Blessed Virgin Mary, his Mother, we too may come to the joys of life everlasting.

Traditional Easter antiphon to the Virgin

Imagine if you can Mary's joy on Easter morn, when she saw the same Divine Seed she had borne within herself now risen and glorious – *surget sicut lilium*. The grain of wheat falling into her furrow had died (for though he left her womb he never left her heart) and now has burgeoned anew, the first-fruits of a vast harvest.

Ruth Burrows

Just as thick oil cannot burn until a wick has been placed in it, so the warm, burning love of the Father did not shine in the world until his Son, through you, Mary, chosen bride of God, took a human body which can be compared to a wick.

And as the wheat cannot become bread until it has been prepared by various instruments, so the Son of God, who is the nourishment of the angels, did not appear in the shape of bread for our refreshment until his body, in your blessed womb, had been formed with limbs and joints.

And just as wine cannot be carried unless a vessel is prepared in advance, so the grace of the Holy Spirit, which is portrayed by wine, could not be given for our everlasting life until the body of your beloved Son, which is portrayed by a vessel, had been prepared through death and suffering.

St Brigid of Sweden

With certainty is your Son safe and living; Mary, there is no doubt; Jesus himself in his own form came to confirm it.

Now, this was his first appearance; he came to his women-folk; he first fortified the women, he comforted the sad ones.

He came first after his victory to his apostles on Easter Day; he showed his beautiful feet and pierced hands.

On Low Sunday he described (this was no falsehood) the signs of his passion; it is then that he gently removed the doubt from Thomas.

Safe is your living Son who has power over the four seasons: winter, spring, bright-visaged summer, autumn with its fruits.

It is he who makes heat and cold, the King who dies not by decay; his is dew and mist; he is the true prince of a fair kingdom.

It is he who raises the wave from the strand until it submerges the prow of proud ships; it is he who calms the screech of the tempests, who casts a fair calm upon the sea.

It is he who raises a great keen wind that breaks a forest from stout roots; it is he who pleasantly represses it so that it troubles not even a tiny pool.

It is you and your Son whom we speak about that Balaam of yore had prophesied; there would arise a star of great dignity from Jacob.

Jesus is the man who has joyfully arisen in Israel; it is in his name (may you bless it!) that all races have hope.

Blathmac (Irish, *c.*700)

The Feast of Pentecost

Mary, as bride of the Spirit, attains full stature on this feast of Pentecost when the Spirit is poured out upon all gathered in the upper room. She who had allowed herself to be overshadowed by the Spirit at the conception of her Son, is now irradiated, body and soul, by the Spirit in all its fullness.

Mary has remained praying with the apostles throughout the days following the Ascension, and in the midst of the praying community she shares all that is given by the Risen Lord to those who love him. Pentecost is the completion of Easter.

In Jewish tradition Pentecost was celebrated seven weeks after Passover. It was a harvest festival, following on after the offering of the first-fruits, which had taken place at the previous feast. Pentecost completed Passover and signalled the end of harvest time.

As a religious celebration Pentecost also commemorated the giving of the Law to Moses on Sinai. It is a great thing to be liberated from slavery, but even more important to understand why and to what end the deliverance has taken place.

The giving of the Law was the high point of the Exodus from Egypt. On Sinai Israel entered into a covenant with God, not just for herself but on behalf of all humanity. Israel was to be a holy nation, a kingdom of priests, a sign of God's love and fidelity for all the nations to see and marvel at.

The Resurrection too took place at Passover. Christ, the

new Paschal Lamb, was sacrificed and rose again. He is, as St Paul says, the first-fruits and pledge of *our* resurrection and redemption. But the gift of the Spirit is the reason for it all. The Resurrection was so that we could all share the same Spirit that animated Jesus and was only liberated by his life-giving death. We are part of his harvest, those who accept the new law, the new covenant, a sign for all nations who are invited to share the same Spirit with us. That is why Pentecost is called the birthday of the Church and why it is so fitting that Mary was present as mother of the new family of her risen Son.

In Jewish circles even today Pentecost retains something of its harvest festival character. The synagogue is decorated with flowers and foliage, the home enriched with dairy foods, especially milk and honey, as reminders of the Promised Land and of the Law 'sweeter than honey and the honeycomb'. The service focuses on the Covenant, and the Scripture readings are on the theme of Sinai. Hymns are sung rejoicing in the gift that the Law has been to the Jewish people, and the fidelity asked of them in return.

All the great feasts of Israel have a special scroll to be read in full during the celebrations. At Passover, it is the Song of Songs which is a spring idyll, a love-song celebrating the desire of God for his chosen people, whom he had delivered from slavery. At Pentecost it is the Book of Ruth, a harvest story, that is in evidence.

Ruth is a tale of human love, devotion, loyalty with universal implications. Ruth, a foreigner, is integrated into God's people (as the Gentiles would later be integrated into the Church, enabling her to be a worshipping community for Jew and Gentile alike); yet this very 'outsider' is the one destined to become the great-grandmother of King David and ancestress of the promised Messiah.

As much as any woman can be, Ruth is symbolic of the universal, salvific festival of the Christian Pentecost. She is an image of Mary, the Spirit-filled woman – one who forgets herself to go out to others; one who shelters beneath the wings of the Lord as she links her destiny with God's people; one who is 'overshadowed' by Boaz, taken under his protection as he promises to wed her, just as Mary is overshadowed by the Spirit at the Annunciation, the wedding of God with our humanity.

The Spirit of Jesus is a Spirit of love. In the person of Ruth we see a selfless, loving woman, model of outgoing 'gift-love' rather than 'need-love'.

In the Book of Ruth we see too the Spirit working through every-day experiences and relationships so as to accomplish the Divine purpose. The Spirit is present, not somewhere 'out there', but right within the very heart of what is happening on the human plane.

As the Spirit-filled woman, Mary too is with us as we live our daily lives, praying with us and for us, that we, like her, may continue with others in prayer, being sensitive to the Spirit's presence in all that happens.

'Let love light up our mortal frame
'Til others catch the living flame.'

* * *

Then afterward I will pour out my spirit on all flesh;
your sons and your daughters shall prophesy,
your old men shall dream dreams,
and your young men shall see visions.
Even on your male and female slaves,
in those days I will pour out my spirit.

Joel 2:28–29

The Feast of Pentecost

On the last day of the festival, the great day, while Jesus was standing there he cried out, 'Let anyone who is thirsty come to me, and let the one who believes in me, drink. As the Scripture has said, "Out of the believer's heart shall flow rivers of living water".' Now he said this about the Spirit, which believers in him were to receive; for as yet there was no Spirit, because Jesus was not yet glorified.

John 7:37–39

All [the apostles] were constantly devoting themselves to prayer, together with certain women, including Mary, the mother of Jesus, as well as his brothers ...

When the day of Pentecost had come, they were all together in one place. And suddenly from heaven there came a sound like the rush of a violent wind, and it filled the entire house where they were sitting. Divided tongues, as it were of fire, appeared among them, and a tongue rested on each of them. All of them were filled with the Holy Spirit and began to speak in other languages, as the Spirit gave them ability.

Acts 1:14; 2:1–4

Now, at the first dawn of the Church, at the beginning of the long journey through faith which began at Pentecost in Jerusalem, Mary was with all those who were the seed of the 'new Israel'. She was present among them as the exceptional witness to the mystery of Christ. And the Church was assiduous in prayer together with her, and at the same time 'contemplated in her the light of the Word made man'. It was always to be so. For when the Church enters more intimately into the supreme mystery of the Incarnation, she thinks of the Mother of Christ with profound reverence and devotion. Mary belongs indissolubly to the mystery of Christ, and she belongs also to the mystery of the Church from the beginning, from the day of the Church's birth. At the basis of what the Church has been from the beginning, and of what she continually must become from generation to generation, in the midst of all the nations, we find the one 'who believed that there would be a fulfilment of what was spoken to her from the Lord'. It is precisely Mary's faith which marks the beginning of the new and eternal Covenant of God with humanity in Jesus Christ. This heroic faith of hers preceded the apostolic witness of the Church, and ever remains in the Church's heart, hidden like a special heritage of God's revelation. All those who from generation to generation accept the apostolic witness of the Church share in that mysterious inheritance, and in a sense share in Mary's faith.

Pope John Paul II

Mary was among those upon whom the Holy Spirit descended. The Gospel specifically says this, and we may perhaps surmise a little of what the gift accompanied by the roar of the divine wind and the flames must have meant to her. As often as the Gospel speaks of her, we may sense some slight remoteness between the human mother and the mystery of her divine Son. The sentence: 'And they did not understand the word that he spoke to them' may serve as an illustration. And now with the coming of the Holy Spirit, all is perfectly clear. No perplexities could remain and every event had its meaning . . .

When the Holy Spirit descended on the disciples he equipped them for their mighty work. When at the same time he came to Mary, her work was already accomplished. All that remained to do was for her to bring all to fuller understanding. From then on she must have lived in ineffable clarity, in indescribable peace. Waiting perhaps for the hour when her Son would call, but in this waiting there was a sense of complete fulfilment. She would have waited a hundred years as well as one day in peace. From this pure stillness, her words must have fallen like rays of light into the hearts of those who came to her to learn of Jesus . . .

The picture of Mary's later life serves as a promise and security. It shows us that we must not take time too seriously, for if we have faith, eternity dwells in us; that we must not overrate the calamities of life, for 'the sufferings of this present time are not worthy to be compared with the glory to come that will be revealed in us', and that we must ask God to show us that eternity dwells in the heart of time.

Romano Guardini

A Song to Mary

> You glowing, most green, verdant sprout,
> in the movement of the Spirit,
> in the midst of wise and holy seekers,
> you bud forth into light.
>
> Your time to blossom has come.
>
> Balsam scented,
> in you the beautiful flower blossomed
>
> It is the beautiful flower
> that lends its scent
> to those herbs,
> and all that had shrivelled and wilted.
>
> It brings them lush greenness once more.

Hildegard of Bingen

'Whoever is joined to the Lord is one spirit with the Lord;' and therefore the operations of the soul in the state of union are the operations of the Holy Spirit, and, consequently, divine . . .

So it was with the glorious Mother of God. Perfect from the first, there was no impression of created things on her soul to turn her aside from God, or in any way to influence her; for her every movement proceeded from the Holy Spirit.

St John of the Cross

My soul trembles and is afraid when I consider the glory of the Mother of God.

She put not in writing the tale of her soul's affliction, and we know little of her life on earth. Her heart, her every thought, her entire soul were wrapped in the Lord; but to her was given something further: she loved humankind and prayed ardently for people, for newly-converted Christians that the Lord might sustain them, and for the whole world that all might be saved. This prayer was her joy and comfort on earth.

We cannot fathom the depth of the love of the Mother of God, but this we know:

The fuller the love, the fuller the knowledge of God.

The more ardent the love, the more fervent the prayer.

The more perfect the love, the holier the life . . .

That Mary did not die of sorrow at the Passion of Christ was only because the strength of the Lord sustained her, for it was his desire that she should behold his Resurrection and live on after the Ascension to be the comfort and joy of the apostles and the new Christian people.

Staretz Silhouan

Let us ask the Blessed Virgin to help us to give the Holy
Spirit the faithfulness he expects of us. May she fortify our
faith which is so weak; faith that must grope through the
darkness and go beyond all anguish to reach God and
believe in him.

Let us say:

Here and now I give you all the love you expect of me;
today and tomorrow,
'til my last breath,
may I be true to this fidelity of love.

Henri Grialou

Hail, O Lady, holy Queen,
Mary, holy Mother of God:
you are the Virgin made Church,
and the one chosen by the most holy Father in heaven
whom he consecrated with his most holy beloved Son
and with the Holy Spirit the Paraclete,
in whom there was and is
all the fullness of grace and every good.
Hail, his Palace!
Hail, his Tabernacle!
Hail, his Home!
Hail, his Robe!
Hail, his Servant!
Hail, his Mother!
And hail all you holy virtues
which through the grace and light of the Holy Spirit
are poured into the hearts of the faithful
so that from their faithless state
you may make them faithful to God.

St Francis of Assisi

O Jesus living in Mary,
come to live in your servants,
with your Spirit of holiness,
in the fullness of your power,
in the perfection of your ways,
in the truth of your virtues,
and in the communion of your divine mysteries.

In your Spirit
and for the glory of God the Father,
overcome every hostile power! Amen

Jean Olier, 1657

I beg you, O I beg you holy Virgin,
that I may have Jesus from that Spirit
through whom you bore Jesus.
Through that Spirit may my soul receive Jesus
through whom your flesh conceived the very same
    Jesus.
By that Spirit let me know Jesus
whereby you yourself were given to know,
to have in your care,
and to give birth to Jesus.
In that spirit let me in my lowliness
speak wonderful things of Jesus,
for in that spirit you confessed yourself
to be the handmaid of the Lord,
desiring it to be done to you
according to the words of the angel.
In that Spirit may I love Jesus
whom you, from now on,
adore as Lord but gaze on as Son.

Ildefonsus of Toledo

May 31

The Visitation

The Visitation seems to be one of the richest mysteries to meditate on in Our Lady's life, for in her *Magnificat* she summarizes the themes of Luke's Gospel. This is a feast of gladness – gladness at the coming of Christ, not only to Mary at the Annunciation, but also to others. Mary brings her child-in-embryo to the formerly barren Elizabeth, that both may rejoice in God's mercy.

This mystery is linked too with Pentecost, feast of the Spirit; for it is the Spirit who impels us away from self and towards others that we may share what we have been given. The life of the Spirit inspires us to break through the self-centred shell which encloses us in misery, and opens us out to live our own personal *Magnificat* with joy.

It isn't that all was easy for Mary at the Visitation. She was in the position of an unmarried mother, without any guarantee for her future except her unshakeable trust in God's promises. No doubt she not only wanted to support her cousin but to receive support in return. Hers is not a song of self-exaltation but of humility. She personifies the Lukan beatitudes which emphasize Jesus as friend of the poor, the outcast, the rejected. That is why the Magnificat has become the theme song of the oppressed peoples of Latin America.

'Blessed is she who believed,' cries Elizabeth as her cousin approaches, thus acknowledging Mary's true greatness as a 'poor one' who relies wholly on God, for then God can work in her all he wills and use her as an instrument to bring his compassionate concern to her friends and neighbours.

The Visitation is a mystery set between the Annunciation and the birth of Christ like a shining jewel. Mary bears her precious burden to another woman, oblivious of her own privilege. Rather, it is the other, sensitive to Mary's new radiance, the radiance that often characterizes pregnant women, making them glow with their inner secret, who acclaims her as the mother of the promised Messiah. 'How is it that the mother of my Lord should come to me?'

Elizabeth 'sees' what Mary cannot see. And so often this is the way it is with us. We do some kind act, accomplish some duty with no thought of the impression we are making. It is the other who discerns the Lord's presence within us, and we are then awakened to the wonder that we are bearers of God's life and love. Truly, the Lord has done great things in our own life, despite our apparent failures and setbacks.

Mary cries out from sheer happiness when Elizabeth blesses her. She knows that God has done *everything* for her. The total poverty of her virginity has been made fruitful. Mary, daughter of Sion, the erstwhile 'forsaken one', is she who is now the image of the all-inclusive New Israel.

> Sing, O barren one who did not bear;
> Break forth into singing and cry aloud,
> you who have not been in travail!
> For the children of the desolate one will be more
> than the children of her that is married, says the
>   Lord . . .

For you will spread abroad to the right and to the
  left,
and your descendants will possess the nations.
For your Maker is your husband
and the Holy One of Israel is your Redeemer.

Isaiah 54:1-5

What a witness there is in joy and gratitude! How we can
overlook these basic attitudes of Mary! Wholly committed
as she is to the mystery of her vocation, in the *Magnificat*
she summarizes God's loving mercy to her personally, and
through her to Israel and to the world. Gratitude is a
component of humble prayer. Gratitude lives in the real
world, the world of what is, what God gives in the concrete
circumstances of life. Gratitude unifies past and present –
in fact, to recount God's mercies is to make them present
now, for his love never changes.

Mary rejoices and gives thanks because God is with her
and calls her to communicate his presence to others. What
more could she want?

We are made to receive love and so diffuse love. Above
all we need to receive and diffuse Christ, who is love.
The world needs Christians who bring spring out of dark
winter, fruitfulness out of barrenness. Mary on her journey
to Elizabeth, Mary the pilgrim Virgin, is our inspiration
as we go forth to meet human needs, to bring help, and
above all, to bring Jesus.

* * *

The voice of my beloved! Behold he comes,
leaping over the mountains, bounding over the hills.
My beloved speaks and says to me:
'Arise, my love, my fair one, and come away;

for now the winter is past, the rain is over and
  gone.
The flowers appear on earth; the time of singing has
  come,
and the voice of the turtledove is heard in our land.
The fig tree puts forth its figs,
and the vines are in blossom: they give forth
  fragrance.
Arise, my love, my fair one, and come away.

Song of Songs 2:8,10−13

In those days Mary set out and went with haste to a Judean town in the hill country, where she entered the house of Zechariah and greeted Elizabeth. When Elizabeth heard Mary's greeting, the child leaped in her womb. And Elizabeth was filled with the Holy Spirit and exclaimed with a loud cry, 'Blessed are you among women, and blessed is the fruit of your womb. And why has this happened to me, that the mother of my Lord comes to me? For as soon as I heard the sound of your greeting, the child in my womb leaped for joy. And blessed is she who believed that there would be a fulfilment of what was spoken to her by the Lord.'
  And Mary said,
  'My soul magnifies the Lord,
  and my spirit rejoices in God my Saviour.'

Luke 1:39−47

How lyrical that is, the opening sentence of St Luke's description of the Visitation. We can feel the rush of warmth and kindness, the sudden urgency of love that sent that girl hurrying over the hills. 'Those days' on which she rose on that impulse were the days in which Christ was being formed in her, the impulse was his impulse . . .

If Christ is growing in us, if we are at peace, recollected, because we know that however insignificant our life seems to be, from it he is forming himself; if we go with eager wills 'in haste', to wherever our circumstances compel us, because we believe he desires to be in that place, we shall find we are driven more and more to act on the impulse of his love.

And the answer to those impulses we shall get from others will be an awakening into life, or the leap into joy of the already wakened life within them . . .

We must be swift to obey the winged impulses of his love, carrying him to wherever he longs to be; and those who recognize his presence will be stirred, like Elizabeth, with new life. They will know his presence, not by any special beauty or power shown by us, but in the way that a bud knows the presence of the light, by an infolding in themselves, a putting forth of their own beauty.

It seems that this is Christ's favourite way of being known, not by his own human features, but by the quickening of his own life in the heart, which is the response to his coming.

Caryll Houselander

Oh, if you could feel in some way
the quality and intensity of the fire sent from heaven,
the refreshing coolness that accompanied it,
the consolation it imparted;
if you could realize the great exaltation of the Virgin
   Mother,

the ennobling of the human race,
the condescension of the divine majesty;
if you could hear the Virgin singing with joy;
if you could go with your Lady
into the mountainous region;
if you could see the sweet embrace
of the Virgin and the woman who had been sterile
and hear the greeting
in which the tiny servant recognized his Lord,
the herald his Judge
and the voice his Word,
then I am sure
you would sing in sweet tones
with the Blessed Virgin
that sacred hymn:
My soul magnifies the Lord . . . ;
and with the tiny prophet
you would exalt, rejoice and adore
the marvellous virginal conception.

St Bonaventure

Whither, O Shepherdess
alone on the mount?
Who bears the sun
fears not the night.

Whither, O Mary,
spouse of God,
glorious Mother
of him who formed you?

What shall you do when the day sets
and, on the mountain,
night o'ertakes you?

Who bears the sun
fears not the night.

The very stars
do stun my sight,
yet brighter your eyes
than them by far.

Already, with you,
the night strides forth;
before your beauty
light fades away.

Who bears the sun
fears not the night.

Lope de Vega Carpio, 1613

The Virgin Mary has always been proposed to the faithful by the Church as an example to be imitated not precisely in the type of life she led, and much less for the socio-cultural background in which she lived and which today scarcely exists anywhere. She is held up to the faithful rather for the way in which, in her own particular life, she fully and responsibly accepted the will of God, because she heard the word of God and acted on it, and because charity and a spirit of service were the driving force of her actions. She is worthy of imitation because she was the first and the most perfect of Christ's disciples. All this has permanent and universal exemplary value.

Pope Paul VI

Mary,
God delights in you so much,
God was so taken with you,
he sank his love's fire
deep within you.

So much love he gave you,
that with it you nurture his Son.

So full of ecstasy is your body
that it resounds with heaven's symphony.

Your womb exults.

It exults like the grass,
grass the dew has nestled on,
grass the dew has infused with verdant strength.

That is how it is with you,
Mother of all joy.

                                        Hildegard of Bingen

My soul is filled with joy as I sing to God my Saviour; He
has looked upon his servant, he has visited his people.

And holy is his name through all generations! Everlasting is his mercy to the people he has chosen, and holy is his name.

I am lowly as a child, but I know from this day forward
that my name will be remembered, all the world will call
me blessèd.

And holy is his name . . .

I proclaim the power of God! He does marvels for his
servants; though he scatters the proud-hearted and destroys
the might of princes.

And holy is his name . . .

To the hungry he gives food, sends the rich away empty.
In his mercy he is mindful of the people he has chosen.
  And holy is his name . . .

In his love he now fulfills what he promised to our fore-
bears. I will praise the Lord my saviour; everlasting is his
mercy.
  And holy is his name . . .

Magnificat paraphrase. Anon

The Immaculate Heart of Mary

The Commemoration of the Immaculate Heart of Mary has been kept on various dates in the past, but is now fixed on the Saturday following the day on which the Sacred Heart of Jesus her Son is solemnly venerated. The original title of the feast was that of 'the most pure heart of Mary', and it was entwined with the rise of devotion to the Sacred Heart of Jesus in the seventeenth century, so that Mother and Son might be venerated together.

In the Bible, the heart denotes the inmost centre of the person, what we might term in psychological language 'the deepest self'. God asks for a worship that springs from our depths, he is not satisfied with mere outward observance. The pure in heart will see God, as Jesus says, while those whose hearts are divided and impure will live divided and fragmented lives, for their being is not unified. Our outward way of acting reflects our inner self; it reveals whether our depth is basically united or fragmentary, selfish or loving.

The whole being of Christ was unified by his total devotion to the Father and the Father's will, and this was reflected in his active love for us. In Jesus we see who the Father is, and how much he loves us. His heart is the symbol of infinite love made visible and tangible in a way we can understand.

Jesus invited those he encountered to learn of him

because he was meek and humble of heart; and at the crucifixion that same heart was pierced to release the Spirit, by means of the blood and water flowing from his side.

The feast of the Heart of Jesus then is basically a feast to celebrate the deepest inner reality of Jesus under the symbol of his heart. The early Fathers of the Church, and later the great medieval mystics, men and women like St Bernard, St Gertrude, St Mechtilde and Julian of Norwich, rejoiced in contemplating the wound in the side of Christ. In the wounds and the blood of the Redeemer they saw his body as if it were adorned with rubies, with shining stars. The wounds became the red crosses emblazoned on the banners of pilgrims and crusaders as they flocked to the Holy Land to venerate the Holy Sepulchre. It was a devotion that carried a note of joy and exaltation.

Devotion to the Heart of Jesus as we have it now, owes much to St John Eudes (d. 1680) who initiated veneration of the combined hearts of Jesus and Mary, and to the revelations made to St Margaret Mary Alacoque (d. 1690). Here there is a stress on sorrow and reparation rather than joy. This is the Heart that has loved us so much and is so little loved in return.

The veneration of the heart of Mary, as with that of Jesus, is a way of representing visually the love that sprang from Mary's inner being; her purity, her compassion, her own meekness and humility, which must have reflected the meekness and humility of her Son. When the Gospel says that Mary 'kept all these things in her heart' we are invited to meditate on the interior, contemplative attitude which penetrates to the depths of the mystery of redemption and is not satisfied with a faith that remains on the surface of life. The more Mary pondered on the mystery of Jesus, his words and actions, the more she could draw from them inspiration and life.

The heart of Mary, as symbol of her self, is a call to us to greater purity, greater knowledge of God, a more interior disposition. How difficult it can be to listen to the Lord who is leading us within. How little we know our true selves, our heart, how seldom we take time to plumb the depths of our capacity for God. And yet each person has that capacity – *carpax Dei* – it is what makes us human.

The purer and more sensitive we become the more we shall begin to live from the mysterious hidden depths we have within us. Our heart is made to be the dwelling place of God, as was Mary's. Her heart is a masterpiece of God's creation. And as we love the whole person of Jesus under the image of his heart, so we can love Mary under the image of hers.

* * *

Hear, O Israel: the Lord is our God, the Lord alone. You shall love the Lord your God with all your heart, and with all your soul, and with all your might. Keep these words that I am commanding you today in your heart. Recite them to your children and talk about them when you are at home and when you are away, when you lie down and when you rise.

Deuteronomy 6:4–7

My child, give me your heart,
and let your eyes observe my ways.

Proverbs 23:26

Set me as a seal upon your heart,
as a seal upon your arm;
for love is strong as death,
passion fierce as the grave.
Its flashes are flashes of fire,
a raging flame.
Many waters cannot quench love,
neither can floods drown it.

Song of Songs 8:6–7

He went down with them and came to Nazareth, and was obedient to them. His mother treasured all these things in her heart.

Luke 2:51

After Jesus Christ, of course, and as far away as the infinite is from the finite, there exists a created being who was always the 'praise of glory' of the most Holy Trinity. She corresponded fully to the divine vocation of which the apostle speaks; she was always holy, unspotted, blameless in the sight of the thrice holy God.

Her soul is so simple, its movements so profound that they cannot be detected; she seems to reproduce on earth the life of the Divinity, the simple Being. And she is so transparent, so luminous that she might be taken for the light itself. Yet she is but the mirror of the Sun of Justice.

'His Mother kept all these words in her heart.' Her whole history can be summed up in these few words. It was within her own heart that she dwelt, and so deeply did she enter it that no human eye could follow her. When I read in the Gospel that Mary 'went into the hill country with haste into a city of Juda' to perform her charitable office to her

cousin Elizabeth, I picture her to myself as she passes –
beautiful, calm, majestic, absorbed in communion with the
Word of God within her. Her prayer, like his, was always;
'*Ecce* – here I am!' Who? 'The handmaid of the Lord,' the
last of his creatures, she, his Mother!

Her humility was so genuine! For she was always forget-
ful of self, unconscious of self, delivered from self. So she
could sing: 'He that is mighty has done great things for
me; henceforth all generations shall call me blessed.'

Elizabeth of the Trinity

God is love, and so that we may have some idea of this
love, he gives a share of it to mothers. The heart of a
mother with her unwearying tenderness, the constancy of
her solicitude, the inexhaustible delicacy of her affection,
is a truly divine creation, although God has placed in her
only a spark of his love for us. Yet, however imperfectly
a mother's heart reflects the divine love towards us, God
gives us our mothers to take his place in some manner with
us. He places them at our side, from our cradles, to guide
us, guard us, especially in our earliest years when we have
so much need of tenderness.

Hence imagine the predilection with which the Holy
Trinity fashioned the heart of the Blessed Virgin chosen to
be the Mother of the Incarnate Word. God delighted in
pouring forth love into her heart, in forming it expressly
to love a God-Man.

In Mary's heart were perfectly harmonized the adoration
of a creature towards her God, and the love of a mother
for her only Son.

Dom Marmion

O holy Virgin Mary tell us, your children, of your love on
earth for your Son and your God.

Tell us how your spirit rejoiced in God your Saviour.

Tell us how you looked upon his beautiful face and
reflected that this was the One all the heavenly hosts
wait upon with awe and love.

Tell us what your soul felt when you carried the wondrous
Babe in your arms.

Tell us how you reared him, how, sick at heart, you and
Joseph sought him three long days in Jerusalem.

Tell us of your agony when the Lord was delivered up to
be crucified and lay dying on the Cross.

Tell us what joy you felt at the Resurrection.

Tell us how your soul yearned after the Ascension of the Lord.

We long to know your life on earth with the Lord but you
were not minded to commit all these things to writing.
Instead, you veiled your secret heart in silence.

Staretz Silhouan

If the early Christians were described as having one heart
and soul, on account of their perfect mutual love; if St Paul
was alive to self no longer, but Christ lived in him, by reason
of the close union of heart between him and his Master, so
that his soul's real life was no longer in the human heart it
animated, but in the Saviour's heart it loved – how much
truer it is to say, God knows, that the Blessed Virgin and
her Son had only one heart, one soul, one life; that his holy
Mother was living, though not with her own life . . . Christ
was alive in her!

Here was actual interpenetration of heart, soul and life
between this Mother and that Son.

St Francis de Sales

The Immaculate Heart of Mary

It is necessary that the Saviour
born of a Virgin without blemish
would be received by an uncorrupted heart:
and as Mary bore him chastely,
so does our soul
guard him without sin.
Mary is the model of such souls.
Since Christ,
as he sought the virginity of his Mother,
thus entirely seeks our souls.

> Maximus of Turin,
> Fourth–Fifth centuries

O Mary, you are the good ground on which the seed
    fell.
You have brought forth fruit a hundredfold.
Draw us close to your loving heart
and keep us there in gentle lowliness and perfect trust.
Teach us to receive the Sacred Word,
to ponder it in silence and yield a rich harvest.
Teach us to be apostles of love.

> Ruth Burrows

O Blessed Virgin Mary, my Queen,
I will praise and honour you through the most gentle
    Heart
of our Lord Jesus Christ, God's Son and yours.
By the love of your pure heart for Jesus Christ,
and by the incomparable pains your heart endured on
    his account,
I ask you to adopt me as your child
and to take me under your maternal protection.

Make me love you,
and may your maternal heart keep and defend me!
During this day, it is my intention to praise, honour
   and venerate you;
and to this end I place all my actions in your pure
   hands
and in your most loving heart.
All that needs correcting, supplying for and making
   perfect,
supply and make perfect for me.
And offer all to the heart of your Son,
into which I pray you to lead me;
that there I may take my rest now and ever,
and especially at the hour of my death.

Michael of Coutances,
Carthusian, Sixteenth century

Heart of Mary, tender heart and pure,
Like thy Son, a refuge safe and sure,
Hail, thou source of life, to sin unknown,
Mirror clear, reflecting God alone;
Save and heal a world by sin o'erthrown.

Heart of Mary, brighter than the sun,
Temple of God in which his will was done,
Throne of light whence Christ was pleased to reign,
Lily fair, untouched by spot or stain,
Ark prepared the Godhead to contain.

Heart of Mary, heart inspiring love,
Pity us and help from heaven above.
Hope art thou of souls whose course is run,
Strength and comfort to each sorrowing one,
Pray for mercy! O beseech thy Son!

The Immaculate Heart of Mary

Heart of Mary, exiles' most sure guide,
Give our hearts to him who for us died;
Sinners' hope, the Word's first earthly shrine,
Open wide heaven's gate and call us thine,
Mother, lead us to thy Son Divine.

From the German

July 16

Our Lady of Mount Carmel

Mount Carmel, in the north of Israel, rises above the Mediterranean Sea, with the modern city of Haifa at its base. Since biblical times Carmel has been renowned for its beauty and verdure (the name means 'garden land'), and was deemed to be a mountain specially dear to God because it witnessed the confrontation of the prophet Elijah with the priests of Baal, when Elijah vindicated the power of the God of Israel over paganism.

Mount Carmel can be seen from the hills surrounding Nazareth and would have been familiar to Jesus, though there is no record of his visiting the place. In fact it is unlikely that he did so, since in New Testament times the mountain was given over to pagan cults. However, it always remained sacred in Jewish tradition on account of its Elijan memories. Later, Christians saw in the little cloud Elijah noticed rising out of the sea and heralding rain after a long drought, an image of the Virgin Mary who, as Mother of the Saviour, carried the One who would bring new life and hope to a thirsting world.

During the time of the Crusades, when Palestine was once more open to pilgrims, a community of Christian hermits from the West settled on the mountain, and in the early thirteenth century obtained a simple Rule from the Patriarch of Jerusalem, St Albert Avogadro. They looked to Elijah as their model, and built their first chapel in honour of the Blessed Virgin Mary, to whom they were especially devoted, becoming known as the brothers of St Mary of Mount Carmel.

As the situation in Palestine became more precarious the hermits began to migrate westwards to their countries of origin, and in 1242 a group came to England and established houses at Hulne in Northumberland and Aylesford in Kent. Here at Aylesford it was decided by an international gathering of brothers to adapt the original Rule and bring it more into line with that of other mendicant Orders such as the Franciscans and Dominicans. The Carmelite Rule nevertheless retained its specific orientation to prayer, heritage of its earliest days, and the brothers' lives continued to be marked by a special devotion to Mary.

It was an Englishman, St Simon Stock, who was instrumental in enabling this adaptation of the Carmelites to the European scene, without which the small Order might well have died out in its new surroundings. Simon was renowned for his love of Our Lady, and later legend attributed to him a vision in which she touched his religious habit and promised to care for all who wore this garment in her honour.

Our Lady of Mount Carmel is then a title for Our Lady which symbolizes the life of prayer proper to Carmel, and rejoices in her protection. The feast itself originated in England in the fourteenth century as an act of thanksgiving for Mary's blessings on the Order, which liked to think of itself as her own. Later the feast spread from England to all Carmelites of whatever country, and was eventually extended to the universal Church. It has been popularized by the many lay people who also wear the Carmelite scapular as a sign of their devotion to Mary under her title Mother of Carmel.

Originally the scapular was a part of every religious habit. It consisted of two straight pieces of material that hung straight down over the shoulders front and back, and was considered symbolic of the sweet yoke of Christ that was taken on when a religious made his or her vows. But in Carmel, through St Simon Stock, the scapular attained special significance as a sign of Mary's benevolence, and was considered to be 'her garment' by those who wore it.

The giving of a garment is a simple act of love that a mother bestows on her children. Mary would have wrapped Jesus in his swaddling bands, prepared the tunics and prayer shawls he needed as he grew up, and woven the unseamed cloak that the soldiers threw lots for at the crucifixion. So the scapular, for those who wear it, is a sign of Mary's motherly care and protection in their daily lives. She 'clothes' them with her own hands, takes them as her children under a new title of belonging.

Obviously not everyone can wear a full length religious habit, so a smaller version of the scapular has been devised for wearing under ordinary clothes. Many, many people receive this as a sign of their love for Mary, a link with her Order, and a sacramental devotion.

As God comes to us through ordinary things in the Sacraments – bread, wine, oil, water – so he can touch us through something as simple as a garment that symbolizes the virtues of his Mother. Mary is never far away. She is as close as our clothing, as practical as prayer-in-action.

* * *

I lift up my eyes to the hills!
from where will my help come?
My help comes from the Lord,
who made heaven and earth.

He will not let your foot be moved;
he who keeps you will not slumber.
He who keeps Israel
will neither slumber nor sleep.

Psalm 121:1–4

Let the wilderness and the dry land exult,
let the wasteland rejoice and bloom,
let it bring forth flowers like the jonquil,
let it rejoice and sing for joy.
The glory of Lebanon is bestowed on it,
the splendour of Carmel and Sharon;
they shall see the glory of the Lord,
the splendour of our God.

Isaiah 35:1–2

As Jesus was speaking, a woman in the crowd raised her voice and said, 'Happy the womb that bore you and the breasts you sucked!' But he replied, 'Still happier those who hear the word of God and keep it.'

Luke 11:27–28

If we are to cultivate the mind and heart of Mary, we must be faithful to the dying command of her Son to behold her. She is 'the mirror of fashion and the mould of form' for every soul that is consecrated to her; and if we do not look into that mirror and mould our lives accordingly, we are certain to lose sight of our ideal. Every wearer of the scapular should follow the counsel of the great Carmelite, Bostius: 'May the loving memory of Mary accompany you day and night, wherever you are, wherever you go, in whatever you do. May it be part of your conversation, your recreation, your sorrow and your rest ... You are indeed my heart and my soul, O Virgin Mother.'

Fr Killian Lynch

Mary is the Virgin in prayer. She appears as such in the visit to the mother of the Precursor, when she pours out her soul in expressions glorifying God, and expressions of humility, faith and hope. This prayer is the Magnificat, Mary's prayer *par excellence*, the song of the Messianic times in which there mingles the joy of the ancient and new Israel. As St Irenaeus seems to suggest, it is in Mary's canticle that there was heard once more the rejoicing of Abraham who foresaw the Messiah, and there rang out in prophetic anticipation the voice of the Church: 'In her exultation Mary prophetically declared in the name of the Church: "My soul proclaims the greatness of the Lord ..." ' And in fact, Mary's hymn has spread far and wide and has become the prayer of the whole Church in all ages.

At Cana, Mary appears once more as the Virgin in prayer: when she tactfully told her Son of a temporal need, she also obtained an effect of grace, namely, that Jesus, in working the first of his 'signs', confirmed his disciples' faith in him.

Likewise, the last description of Mary's life presents her as praying. The apostles 'joined in continuous prayer, together with several women, including Mary the Mother of Jesus and with his brothers.' We have here the powerful presence of Mary in the early Church and in the Church throughout all ages, for, having been assumed into heaven, she has not abandoned the mission of intercession and salvation. The title Virgin in prayer also fits the Church, which day by day presents to the Father the needs of her children, praises the Lord unceasingly and intercedes for the salvation of the world.

Pope Paul IV

Virgin of the Incarnation,
In the mysteries of grace
God has made his habitation
In our soul's most secret place.
Towards that bright and inner kingdom
All our words and ways compel
For the Father, Son and Spirit
In its sacred silence dwell.

Queen and beauty of Mount Carmel,
Virgin of the solitude,
In the wilderness of Carmel
Lies the world's eternal good.
Draw us into deep seclusion
And make God alone our goal,
In the mystical Mount Carmel
That lies hidden in the soul.

Jessica Powers

Pure as Carmel's snows and lovely
As the first fair morning shine,
Crowned with stars of changeless splendour,
Hail, thou Mother-Maid divine!
Hail, thou lady of the Mountain
Rearing up its stately height,
Emblematic of thy graces,
Glowing in immortal light.
Mother of Mount Carmel, hear!
Shades are falling, night is near!

From the wide wastes of the ocean
Where the bird-like vessels sail,
From the deep haunts of the city
Where the weak and tempted wail,
In the chapel, in the battle,
From the bondsman and the free,
This sweet incense still is wafted,
This sweet prayer swept up to thee.
Mother of Mount Carmel, hear!
Shades are falling, night is near.

Traditional

Flower of Carmel, vine with blossoms weighed,
Shining light of heaven, bearing Child though maid,
None like to thee.

Mother most tender, whom no man didst know,
On all Carmel's children thy favour bestow,
Star of the sea.

Flos Carmeli
(Traditional)

Bounteous Mother of God,
Glory of Mount Carmel,
we are members of your family;
endow us with your own virtues;
have pity, and protect us
from every danger.

Traditional

If every morning you were to kiss the scapular saying;
'Mother of God, use me today,' she would use you. You
have only to put the intention in the very centre of your

will and you will become 'a living tool of God'. It is very simple. Even children will understand and practise it. They are the world's greatest realists and make wonderful apostles.

Fr Malachy Lynch of Aylesford

May God, who set apart the Carmelite Order
for the honour of the Blessed Virgin Mary,
clothe you with her virtues and make you worthy of
    her service.

May he who endowed Carmel
with the spirit of the prophet Elijah,
make you fervent in prayer and zealous for his
    honour.

May he who has blessed Carmel
with a host of saintly sons and daughters,
make you their worthy brothers and sisters on earth
and partakers of their everlasting fellowship in
    heaven.

Blessing: Carmelite Missal

Father,
may the prayers of the Blessed Virgin Mary,
Mother and Queen of Carmel,
protect us, and bring us
to your holy Mountain, Christ our Lord,
who lives and reigns with you and the Holy Spirit,
one God, for ever and ever. Amen.

Carmelite Breviary

July 26

Sts Joachim and Anne, Parents of Mary

The commemoration of the parents of Mary reminds us that she, like all of us, came from a particular background and heritage, which prepared her for her particular task in the world.

Scripture has nothing to say of Mary's parents, not even their names are recorded. Tradition, however, has designated them as Joachim and Anne, and as such they are written of in the apocryphal gospels. Joachim is a Latin form of the name Heli (Eliakim) given to Joseph's father in the Lukan genealogy, while Anne is named for Hannah (Anna) the mother of Samuel who, in her barrenness, prayed for a child who would be consecrated to God from birth. In the Apocrypha the story goes that, like so many parents of special children in the Bible, Joachim and Anne were barren, and Mary was an answer to prayer, an infant welcomed in their old age when all hope had been lost.

What kernel of truth (if any) is in these legends is debatable. But, as the name Anne signifies 'grace', so Mary, as a child of grace, is the daughter given to her parents as gift, just as is every child born into the world. During the Middle Ages devotion to St Anne was extremely popular, and there were many images made of her with Mary at her knee learning the Scriptures; or of Anne with two children, one on each arm, to show her relationship to her daughter, Mary, and grandson, Jesus. Mothers identified with Anne, to whom they prayed for a safe delivery during childbirth, and who they hoped would obtain good husbands for their own daughters in their turn.

What we can be sure of is that Mary was brought up in a home where the practices of the Jewish faith were observed and there was an environment conducive to her human and religious development. Much of a girl's successful maturing process depends on a satisfactory mother–daughter bond, and this must have been provided by Anne, enabling Mary in her turn to be sure of her feminine identity and womanly giftedness.

It is perfectly possible that both Joseph and Mary had other brothers and sisters, ensuring that they knew the give and take of sibling interaction in their youth, as well as providing the growing Jesus with multiple family relationships: aunts, uncles and cousins, as well as grandparents. The Gospels explicitly mention Mary's sister, 'Mary the wife of Clopas'. It was not unheard of for two girls in a family to have variants of the same name; or this Mary might have been the wife of one of Mary's brothers, or a relative of Joseph.

The main point of a feast such as this (which, since the reform of the calendar has commemorated Anne and Joachim together instead of separately), is that Jesus existed with many family bonds of various kinds. Grandparents play an important part in a child's unfolding life, and a child without grandparents is deprived of the rich experience gained through closeness to an older generation than just his or her parents.

This feast then makes us remember the blessings of home and family, and the important part they play in the formation of children, bonding young and old together in harmony. And it is also a feast of Mary, when she sees her own parents loved and honoured as she herself must have loved and honoured the couple to whom she owed her life and early education.

* * *

Listen to me your father, O children;
act accordingly, that you may be kept in safety.
For the Lord honours a father above his children,
and he confirms a mother's rights over her children.
Those who honour their father atone for sins,
and those who respect their mother
are like those who lay up a treasure.
Those who honour their father will have joy in their
    own children,
and when they pray they will be heard.

Sirach 3:1 – 5

With all your heart honour your father,
and do not forget the birth-pangs of your mother.
Remember that through your parents you were born,
and what can you give back to them
that equals their gift to you.

Sirach 7:27 – 28

A capable wife who can find?
She is far more precious than jewels.
The heart of her husband trusts in her,
and he will have no lack of gain.
She does him good, and not harm, all the days of her
    life.

*She seeks wool and flax, and works with willing
    hands.
She is like the ships of the merchant,
    she brings her food from far away.
Her husband is known at the city gates,
    taking his seat among the elders of the land.
Strength and dignity are her clothing,
    and she laughs at the time to come.
She opens her mouth with wisdom,
    and the teaching of kindness is on her tongue.
Her children rise up and call her happy;
    her husband too, and he praises her.*

Proverbs 31:10–14,23,25–28

Mary spent her youth in her parents' house. Father and mother are God's appointed educators of a child. Naturally the training of daughters was chiefly the mother's task, and from her a girl learned what she needed for life: cooking, grinding on the hand-mill, baking bread, weaving, spinning, sewing, gathering wood, drawing water, keeping the house clean, the care of the domestic animals, work in the garden and field. Country people had a modest standard of board and lodging. Mary would have to get used to work at an early age, and was surely not pampered. Active work with her parents in house and field, with simple food and rough clothing, would harden her and make her fit to endure the arduous journeys of later days.

Still more important was the religious training. Although Rabbi Eleazar said: 'He who instructs his daughter in the Law is like a man who teaches her unseemly things,' that was certainly not the view of wise parents. Of the chaste Susannah it is written: 'Her parents, being just, had instructed their daughter according to the Law of Moses.'

The synagogue's great merit was that it gave a thorough knowledge of the ancestral religion, and awakened and fostered a deep piety. The people learned to know and appreciate the beauty and wisdom of the sacred books, and were thus armed against the seductions of the paganism that surged all around them. No severer penalty could be inflicted on the Israelite than to be excluded from the synagogue.

Nazareth too had its synagogue, and Mary's parents were no doubt assiduous frequenters of it. With them their daughter too had the opportunity of taking part in the Sabbath service. Again and again she heard read the great promises of a coming Redeemer, and again and again the famous women of the past, such as Ruth, Hannah, Judith, Esther, rose up before her mind . . .

Family life too was sanctified and uplifted by prayer. The family prayed at various times of the day, took part in the great common pilgrimages to the Temple at Jerusalem, and kept the annual round of feasts at home.

J. Patsch

Prayer for the Lighting of the Sabbath Candles

Lord of the Universe,
I am about to perform the sacred duty
of kindling the lights in honour of the Sabbath,
even as it is written:
You shall call the Sabbath a delight,
and the holy day of the Lord honourable.
And may the effect of my fulfilling this commandment
be that a stream of abundant life and heavenly
   blessing

flow in upon me and mine,
and that you would be gracious to us and bless us
and cause your presence to dwell among us.
Father of Mercies, continue your loving kindness
to me and my dear ones.
Make me worthy to rear my children
that they walk in the way of the righteous before you,
loyal to your Law and clinging to good deeds.
Keep far from us all manner of shame, grief and care;
and grant that peace, light and joy ever abide in our
    home.
For with you is the fountain of life;
and in your Light we see light.

Hebrew Prayer Book

It was the mommas, not the missionaries or the mystics or
other religious machos, who bonded me and my generation
into religion.

Rabbi Lionel Blue

The wife and the mother is the radiant sun of the family.
She is the sun by her generosity and gift of self, by her
unfailing readiness, by her watchful and prudent delicacy
in all matters which can add joy to the lives of her husband
and her children. She spreads around her light and warmth.
And if you can say that a marriage augurs well when both
partners seek the happiness of the other rather than their
own, this noble feeling and intention is more especially the
quality of the wife, although it concerns both husband and
wife. It is born of the very pulse of her mother's heart and
its wisdom; that wisdom which, if it receives bitterness,
gives only joy; if it receives belittlement, returns only dig-

nity and respect. It is like the sun, which brightens the cloudy morning with its dawning ray and in its setting gilds the evening shower.

Pope Pius XII

Mr L. offered to Aylesford, in thanksgiving, a beautiful thirteenth-century statue. He had said it was a statue of Our Lady but that she had two children with her, one on each arm. When it was brought it was found to be St Anne with Our Lady on one arm and the Holy Child on the other. This was a museum piece but suddenly it dawned on us that Our Lady was symbolically bringing her mother to us . . .

I am ashamed to say I had never thought of St Anne at all, but you see how that did not make any difference. She is here and need give no thanks to me or to anyone here, but to one of her own race. (Mr L. was Jewish.)

I discovered that there has been a great cultus of St Anne going back a long way and extending even to England. I discovered too that everybody seemed to know a homely rhyming verse, 'Pray, St Anne, get me a man, and any old thing won't do'.

This surely belongs to a time when people knew the saints and what they expected of them.

Fr Malachy Lynch of Aylesford

O most beautiful and sweetest maiden,
O lily, risen among thorns,
grown on the royal and fertile root of David,
through you the sovereignty of priesthood is enriched.
O daughter of Adam, O Mother of God!
Blessed be the womb from which you emerged.

Sts Joachim and Anne, Parents of Mary

Blessed the arms which carried you
and the lips that delighted in your innocent kisses,
the lips of your parents . . .
Today the salvation of the world begins.

St John Damascene, 749

Oh! How radiantly the rising sun shone in Anne's womb
when Mary's body there was brought to life by the coming
of the soul; Mary, whose coming to be angels and humans
had so ardently desired to see!

Just as a good zither player could approve of an unfinished zither if he could foresee it would have a pleasing
tone, so did the Creator of all things greatly love Mary in
her childhood, both in body and in soul, for he knew
beforehand that her words and deeds would please him
more than all beautiful music.

St Bridget of Sweden

Lord, God of our ancestors,
you bestowed on Saint Joachim and Saint Anne
this singular grace
that their daughter, Mary,
should become the mother of your Son, Jesus Christ.
Grant, at their intercession,
the salvation you promised to your people.

Roman Breviary

August 5

Dedication of St Mary Major

Every church keeps its own dedication day with great rejoicing, but this feast of the major basilica in Rome dedicated to Mary has been extended to the whole Church, emphasizing its universal importance.

The basilica of St Mary Major, 'Our Lady of the Snows' is its lovely subsidiary title, stands as a monument to the Council of Ephesus when Mary was acclaimed as Theotokos, Mother of God, and not merely mother of the man Jesus. The dogma of the divine motherhood is central to faith in Christ, and is seen as of great importance in the evolution of the Christian faith.

The designation 'Our Lady of the Snows' refers to a medieval legend, which is rather similar to the legend of the foundation of Walsingham. It is said that the Roman patrician John and his wife wished to honour Mary by devoting their wealth to some work in her honour, since they had no children of their own. The couple prayed that Mary would make her desire known to them, and she obliged with the following miracle. On 5 August, when Rome is usually sweltering under a summer sun, a portion of the Esquiline hill was found covered in snow which had fallen during the night. Meanwhile, that same night John and his wife dreamed separately that they were to build a church dedicated to the Virgin on the site where snow was lying. Pope Liberius, who had had a similar dream, proceeded immediately to the hill and marked out the area on which the proposed church would be built, as indicated by the snowfall.

Later, another church was erected on the same site, and in 432, following the definition of Mary's divine motherhood, was consecrated in her honour under this title. The walls of the building's interior are decorated with beautiful mosaics which are among the oldest known in the Christian world.

St Mary Major contains a permanent grotto, fashioned as a replica of Bethlehem's cave of the nativity, thus earning the church the designation of 'Rome's Bethlehem' or 'St Mary of the Crib'.

Each person is also a church consecrated to God, as Mary was in her motherhood. She has always been seen as an embodiment of the Church, as Bride, Mother and perfect disciple of the Word. The liturgy always makes Mary a bridge to Jesus, not an end in herself.

This is a feast on which to renew our faith in Jesus as true God and true man, born of the Virgin Mary, who is rightly called the Mother of God, her oldest and most venerable title. It is a feast, too, on which to remember that each of us is God's house. Together we build up the Church here on earth and are called, as one body, to eternal beatitude. The Sacraments, foretaste of heaven, are celebrated in consecrated buildings all over the world, whether they are grand basilicas like St Mary Major or the humblest mud hut in missionary lands. God comes to us as we are, where we are, for 'we are his dwelling and his homeliest home' (Julian of Norwich).

* * *

Will God indeed dwell on earth? Even heaven and the highest heaven cannot contain you, much less this house which I have built!

Regard your servant's prayer that your servant prays to you today; that your eyes may be open day and night towards this house, the place where you said, 'My name shall be there,' that you may heed the prayer that your servant prays towards this place.

Hear the plea of your servant and of your people Israel when they pray towards this place; O hear in heaven your dwelling place; heed and forgive.

1 Kings 8:27–30

Like living stones, let yourselves be built into a spiritual house, to be a holy priesthood, to offer spiritual sacrifices to God through Jesus Christ.

1 Peter 2:5

You are no longer strangers and aliens, but you are citizens with the saints and also members of the household of God, built upon the foundation of the apostles and prophets, with Christ Jesus himself as the cornerstone. In him the whole structure is joined together and grows into a holy temple in the Lord; in whom you also are built together spiritually into a dwelling place for God.

Ephesians 2:19–22

One must believe simply and firmly that Mary is truly the Mother of God; yet who can claim to have always faced up to the implications of this affirmation.

It conveys, better than anything else, the truths of the Incarnation, and the Council of Ephesus so devised it. It tells us with rather crude force what is to be believed: that that very Jesus, born of Mary, is truly the eternal Son of the Father.

What we can and must do is make an act of faith – faith in the reality of the Incarnation, in the reality that the Son of God was born of Mary and was faithful unto death to her who bore him. Directly because of this, Mary exists to help us to a deeper belief in the Saviour. She obliges us to rise above the superficiality of a prayer addressed only to herself, when she is but a creature.

The Blessed Virgin calls us to make an act of faith and to consider its implications. That is why it is so good to turn to her and why one is so well off with her. The graciousness that we find there is not simply the presence of human purity and goodness: it is the divine love itself. Faith gives it to us if we are willing to believe.

Mary believed first, and blessed is she among women. It is this blessedness that she invites us to know.

If our acts of faith are rightly made and dependent on her to reach Our Lord, they will certainly send us back to her in gratitude for what she does for us. And all that we have been led to do for her will unfailingly lead us nearer her Son. She is completely maternal in his service. Her love for us with its attentive prayers and reminders leads us more deeply into her Son's Kingdom of love, where she was the first to enter.

Gabriel Cardinal Garrone

The church is like the soul of the people, which soars like this stone building itself, raised by a common intention of prayer and piety, an intention which rises to the vaulted roof, sings and prays, groans and sighs.

The church is built to house the Eucharist, which throbs with life here among the precious stones and metals and the harmonies of worshipping hearts; and it is built for Our Lady whose mild eyes look down from her altars . . .

There are hundreds of cathedrals and churches, many of them dedicated to the glory of Mary, which have risen like miracles of art to enshrine the sacred Host and to express the people's fervent love for the Blessed Sacrament and Our Lady.

Pope John XXIII in the Basilica of St Mary Major

The Church is fruitful,
made holy by the blood of Christ:
a bride made radiant with his glory,
a virgin splendid in the wholeness of her faith,
a mother blessed through the power of the Spirit.

Preface for the Consecration of a Church

Mary is the house and the palace of the Great King, of God himself. Our Lord, the co-equal Son of God, once dwelt in her. He was her guest; nay more than a guest, for a guest comes into a house as well as leaves it. But our Lord was actually *born in this holy house*. He took his flesh and his blood from this house, from the flesh, from the veins of Mary. Rightly then was she made to be of pure gold, because she was to give of that gold to form the body of the Son of God. She was golden in her conception, golden in her birth. She went through the fire of suffering like gold in the furnace, and when she ascended on high, she was, in the words of our hymn,

Above all the angels in glory untold,
Standing next to the King in a vesture of gold.

J. H. Newman

O Mary, immensity of heaven,
foundation of the earth,
depth of the sea, light of the sun,
beauty of the moon,
splendour of the stars in the heavens.
You are greater than the cherubim,
more eminent than the seraphim,
more glorious than the chariots of fire.
Your womb bore God,
before whose majesty mortals stand in awe.
Your lap held the glowing coal.
Your knees supported the lion,
whose majesty is fearful.
Your hands touched
the One who is untouchable,
and the fire of the Divinity which is in him.
Your fingers resemble the glowing tongs
with which the prophet received the coals
of the heavenly oblation.
You are the basket for this bread of ardent flame
and the chalice for this wine.
O Mary, who nurtured in your womb
the fruit of oblation,
we children of this sanctuary
pray to you with perseverance
to guard us from the adversary which ensnares us;
and as the measure of water cannot be parted from
    the wine,
so let us not be separated from you and your Son,
the Lamb of salvation.

Ethiopic Anaphora,
Eighth century

While singing to your Child
we all praise you as a living temple, O Mother of
    God,
for the Lord who holds all things in his hand
dwelt in your womb,
and he sanctified and glorified you,
and taught all to cry to you:

Rejoice, tabernacle of God the Word!
Rejoice, saint greater than the saints!
Rejoice, ark made golden by the Spirit!
Rejoice, inexhaustible treasury of Life!
Rejoice, precious diadem of pious kings!
Rejoice, adorable boast of devoted priests!
Rejoice, unshaken tower of the Church!
Rejoice, impregnable wall of the Kingdom!
Rejoice, through whom we obtain our victories!
Rejoice, before whom our foes fall prostrate!
Rejoice, healing of my body!
Rejoice, salvation of my soul!
Rejoice, unwedded Bride!

Akathist Hymn

We hail the mystery of the Blessed Trinity,
which has called all this our company together to this
    church of Mary, the Mother of God.
Hail Mary, Mother of God, august treasury of the
    whole world,
unquenchable torch,
crown of virginity,
sceptre of orthodoxy, temple indestructible, mother
    and virgin.

Through you is named blest in the holy Gospel
the One who comes in the name of the Lord.
Hail Mary!
You contained the uncontainable in your virginal
    womb.
Through you the Trinity is glorified;
through you is the Cross named precious, and adored
    throughout the world;
through you heaven exults.

St Cyril of Alexandria,
at the Council of Ephesus

August 15

The Assumption

Rise up! the cold winds from earth have departed,
Meadows are striving fragrant flowers to vary,
Praising Our Lady, Mother and Lifebearer,
Rise up O Mary!

Ark made of sweet wood, manna pure containing,
Bread of such virtue and sublime perfection
Quickens the dead bones, calling them from slumber
To resurrection.

Hymn for Assumption Vespers

The Assumption of the Blessed Virgin Mary is one of the oldest celebrations in the Church and merits a vigil Mass as well as a Mass on the day itself. Mary, the ark of the Covenant, the one who bore the Messiah in her womb, has not been left to return to dust, but has gone to join her Son in heaven, body and soul. She is now what we will be in due course. Her flesh even now is glorified and enjoys the vision of God.

Carl Jung saw this dogma as extremely significant. It reveals the importance of the feminine presence, the importance of the body, and indeed of the whole person who is called to participate in the mystery of salvation. Reason alone is not enough. The Assumption is a sign of what we are all destined to attain in the resurrection of our own bodies as proclaimed in the Creed. It is an intuitive feast, springing from what Christians have *felt* about Mary rather than what *rational thought* might tell us. The liturgy is full of poetic bridal symbolism. Mary 'falls asleep' to this life to awaken to the world to come, where she is received into glory by her Son.

This celebration, 'Our Lady in August', is Mary's Easter. She is the woman of our harvest time, when the earth is laden with golden corn, and ripe fruit is waiting to be gathered in.

On the feast of the Transfiguration we recall the glory that shone through the body of Jesus, revealing him as the Christ before he went up to his Passion and death in Jerusalem. In the Assumption, what Mary truly is as Mother of God shines through in her own flesh once her earthly life is over. Pain and sorrow are swallowed up in joyful affirmation of her work completed.

We should never contemplate Mary apart from her Son and in relationship to him. She has nothing purely of herself. All is grace and gift, from the Immaculate Conception to the Assumption. Her whole person is dependent on God, turned Godwards. Now this is made evident to all.

In the Assumption we visualize Mary's 'glory'. Her whole life is affirmed and made radiant, penetrated by the Godhead in every pore of her being.

And what is this feast saying to us? That we too, body and soul, are called to glory. In the end, what we really are, what we have made of our lives during the time given to us below, will shine through in our flesh. What we *are* will be revealed; not what we pretended to be, not the image we tried to project, not our disguises. Everything will be brought to the light, as Jesus says, so that it can be seen whether what was done was done in God or not. With Mary *all* was done in God, in the truth; and so she can glory in life in the light for ever. There is no darkness in her at all.

Our work on earth is to glorify the Father as Jesus did, by finishing the work he gives us to do. Right now so much is hidden, as it was in Mary's life, for she too had to live by faith, not sight. Yet she believed that 'exile ends in glory'.

One day we will see things in their true perspective; but the pure in heart already get a glimpse of the presence of God here on earth. They intuit it in all that happens, and respond appropriately and freely.

Caryll Houselander wrote of an experience she had when travelling on the London Underground. Suddenly it seemed to her that the people she was with in the carriage became suffused with Christ. She saw Christ shining in and radiating through the drab exterior of each one; and she realized that this is actually how people are, each one is radiant with the Christ who dwells within them. It is we who do not see it and are taken up with appearances only, whereas in truth we live 'with inward glory crowned.' And love discovers that glory in the most unlikely places, even the London Underground.

*   *   *

Who is this that looks forth like the dawn,
fair as the moon, bright as the sun,
terrible as an army with banners.

Song of Songs 6:10

You are the glory of Jerusalem, you are the great boast of Israel, you are the honour of our nation.
You have done great good to Israel and God is well pleased with you. May the Almighty Lord bless you for ever.

Judith 15:9–10

For this perishable body must put on imperishability, and this mortal body must put on immortality. When this perishable body puts on imperishability, and this mortal body puts on immortality, then the saying that is written will be fulfilled: 'Death has been swallowed up in victory.'

'Where, O death, is your sting?'

The sting of death is sin, and the power of sin is the law. But thanks be to God, who gives us the victory through our Lord Jesus Christ.

Therefore, my beloved, be steadfast, immovable, always excelling in the work of the Lord, because you know that in the Lord your labour is not in vain.

1 Corinthians 15:53–58

What grace, sweetness and solemnity in the scene of Mary's 'falling asleep', as the Christians of the East image it! She is lying in the serene sleep of death; Jesus stands beside her, and clasps her soul, as if it were a tiny child, to his heart, to indicate the miracle of her immediate resurrection and glorification.

The Christians of the West, raising their eyes and hearts to heaven, choose to portray Mary borne body and soul to the eternal kingdom. The greatest artists saw her thus, incomparable in her divine beauty. Oh let us too go with her, borne aloft by her escort of angels!

This is a source of consolation and faith, in days of grief or pain, for those privileged souls – such as we can all become, if only we respond to grace – whom God is silently preparing for the most beautiful victory of all, the attainment of holiness. The mystery of the Assumption brings home to us the thought of death, of our own death, and gives us a sense of serene confidence; it makes us understand and welcome the thought that the Lord will be, as we would wish him to be, near us in our last agony, to gather into his own hands our immortal soul.

Pope John XXIII

We are told by St Matthew that after Our Lord's death upon the Cross 'the graves were opened, and many bodies of the saints that had slept' – that is, slept the sleep of death - 'arose, and coming out of the tombs after his Resurrection, came into the Holy City, and appeared to many.' St Matthew says, '*many* bodies of the Saints' – that is, the holy prophets, priests and kings of former times – rose again in anticipation of the last day.

Can we suppose that Abraham, or David, or Isaiah, or Ezechiel, should have been thus favoured, and not God's own Mother?

Had she not a claim on the love of her Son to have what any others had? Was she not nearer to him than the greatest of the saints before her? And is it conceivable that the law of the grave should admit of relaxation in their case and not in hers? Therefore we confidently say that Our Lord, having preserved her from sin and the consequences of sin by his Passion, lost no time in pouring out the full merits of that Passion upon her body as well as her soul.

J. H. Newman

In you rejoices, O full of grace, all creation,
the company of angels and all humankind.
O holy temple and spiritual paradise,
O pride of virgins.
Thanks to you, God took flesh becoming a child,
he, our God, foremost of all ages.

Of your womb he has made, in truth, a throne
and formed it greater than the heavens.
In you, O full of grace, all creation rejoices.
Glory to you.

St John Damascene

    Mary,
    O luminous Mother,
    holy, healing art!

    Eve brought sorrow to the soul,
    but by your holy Son
    you pour balm
    on death's wounds and travail.

    You have indeed conquered death!

    You have established life!

    Ask for us life.
    Ask for us radiant joy.
    Ask for us the sweet, delicious ecstasy
    that is for ever yours.

Hildegard of Bingen

Let us rejoice with the Mother of God,
unite in the chorus of angels
and celebrate the feast of feasts:
the Assumption of the Ever-virgin.

On earth she was the treasure and model of virgins;
In heaven she is as one who intercedes for all.
Favourite of God, procuring for us the gifts of the
    Spirit
and with her word teaching wisdom.

The Ever-virgin Mother of God is our earth in
  blossom.
While she was on earth she watched over all.
She was like a universal providence
for all the faithful.
Ascended into heaven, interceding for us,
she became a secure refuge for the human race,
near to her Son and God.

Theotekno of Livia, c.600

On the Glorious Assumption of Our Blessed Lady

Hark! She is call'd. The parting hour is come.
Take thy farewell, poor world! Heav'n must go home.
A piece of heav'nly earth, purer and brighter
Than the chaste stars, whose choice lamps come to
  light her
While through the crystal orbs, clearer than they,
She climbs and makes a far more milky way.
She's called. Hark how the dear immortal dove
Sighs to his silver mate, 'Rise up, my love!
Rise up, my fair, my spotless one!
The winter's past, the rain is gone.
The spring is come, the flowers appear.
No sweets but thou art wanting here.
Come away, my dove! Cast off delay.
The court of Heav'n is come
To wait upon thee home. Come, come away!'

The flowers appear,
Or quickly would, wert thou once here.
The spring is come, or, if it stay,
'Tis to keep time with thy delay.

The Assumption

The rain is gone, except so much as we
Detain in needful tears to weep the want of thee.
The winter's past.
Or, if it make less haste,
His answer is, 'Why, she does so.
If summer come not, how can winter go?' ...

'Maria,' men and angels sing,
'Maria, mother of our King.'
Live, rosy princess live. And may the bright
Crown of a most incomparable light
Embrace thy radiant brows. O may the best
Of everlasting joys bathe thy white breast.
Live, our chaste love, the holy mirth
Of Heav'n, the humble pride of earth
Live, crown of women, queen of men.
Live, mistress of our song. And when
Our weak desires have done their best,
Sweet angels, come and sing the rest.

Richard Crashaw, 1649

Come, O festive angels,
let us prepare ourselves to dance
and to make the church resound with songs
on the occasion of the deposition of God's Ark.

Behold: today heaven throws open its bosom
to receive her who brought forth the Great One;
the earth, receiving the source of life,
covered itself with blessings and beauty.
The angels make a choir with the apostles
and watch over with reverence the Mother
of the King of Life,
who passes from this life to the other.

Let us all kneel before her and pray:
O Queen, do not forget those
who are joined to you by affinity
and celebrate with faith
your holy dormition.

Theophanus, 845

August 22

The Queenship of Mary

The Queenship of Mary falls on the octave day of the Assumption and is closely connected with it. It emphasizes the inner dignity of Mary under the symbol of her crowning. Now in heaven, she is acclaimed and honoured as none other.

But what really constitutes a mother's honour is her children. A mother who celebrates an anniversary with even one of her children absent finds the gathering incomplete. As mother of humanity, Mary's crown is each one of us as brothers and sisters of her Son. Each child in a family is irreplaceable; if one is not there with her, Mary's crown is unfinished.

Each one of us is gifted, each one unique as a child of the Eternal Father. Each one is a king or queen in some way, not in outward splendour but in the call to service, which a royal title implies when it is properly understood.

In reality we do not value ourselves enough, we do not sufficiently believe in our dignity and our call. We feel 'failures', not up to standard when compared with others. Envy and jealousy creep into our relationships. We want to shine and to excel rather than only to be part of the total picture.

In life, self-acceptance is *basic* if we are to grow into maturity. Self-love and self-acceptance lead us to love others and to love God because we are free from the chains which hold us back and keep us entangled in dead-end attitudes.

Anyone can lead a full life, a life full of love, full of God, no matter what their temperamental or physical handicaps.

One person who is a model of self-acceptance and reaching-out love is the monk who wrote some of our most beautiful Marian antiphons: the 'Hail holy Queen' (*Salve Regina*) and the 'Loving Mother of our Redeemer' (*Alma redemptoris mater*). Sometimes you will see these antiphons attributed to Hermann Contractus, or Hermann the Lame. *Contractus* is a far more evocative word and closer to the truth.

Hermann was born, not with ordinary lameness, but with crippling and irremedial deformities. In all his forty-one years of life he was never for a moment without pain. He could neither stand nor walk, and when he sat he could only do so in a chair specially constructed to support his spine. His hands were weak and clumsy, his speech slurred by a cleft palate.

Hermann's parents, both of the German nobility, decided that the only place for their son, one of fifteen children, would be a monastery. There was no other alternative open to them if he was to receive the necessary care. And for Hermann there was no choice at all, except *how* he would cope with the deformities he had been given.

Yet in the monastery of Reichnau, where he was taken as a child, Hermann grew into a saint, fulfilling all his natural and human potential in a way that very few of us manage to do. Physical handicaps can lead to self-rejection, inferiority, but not so in this little monk. He accepted himself completely *as he was*, without rancour or rebellion. His biographer calls him 'friendly, easy to talk to, always laughing, eagerly cheerful, obliging . . .' with the result that, instead of being a burden on the community everybody loved him. He became a community asset, not a liability.

Hermann learned Maths, Astronomy, Science. He read classical authors so that he had interesting conversation to share instead of continually harping on his health problems. He trained his crippled hands to make astrolabes and clocks and musical instruments. He wrote music, a life of Christ, a scientific treatise. He was always doing something to make life pleasant for others, as well as enriching himself in the process.

And the woman he turned to, as he would know no other woman, was Mary, his Queen and mother, his sweetness and his hope. When we realize who wrote this lovely prayer to the Queen of heaven it takes on an added pathos.

No one is so handicapped that God cannot use them. No one is outside the love of Mary for all her children. Hermann could have sulked and complained at his twisted limbs and weak extremities. Instead he is remembered for his holiness; one who makes the crown of the Mother of God shine with splendour.

* * *

Hear, O daughter, consider and incline your ear;
forget your people and your father's house,
and the king will desire your beauty.
Since he is your lord, bow to him;
the people of Tyre will seek your favour with gifts,
the richest of the people with all kinds of wealth.
The princess is decked in her chamber with
*   gold-woven robes;*
in many-coloured robes she is led to the king;
behind her the virgins, her companions, follow.
With joy and gladness they are led along
as they enter the palace of the king.

Psalm 45:10-15

A great portent appeared in heaven: a woman clothed with the sun, with the moon under her feet, and on her head a crown of twelve stars.

Revelation 12:1

Listen! I am standing at the door knocking; if you hear my voice and open the door, I will come in to you and eat with you, and you with me. To the one who conquers I will give a place with me on my throne, just as I myself conquered and sat down with my Father on his throne.

Revelation 3:20–21

Once upon a time I was lifted up, and I was not then in prayer, but I had sat myself down to rest, for it was after dinner. Hence I was not even thinking about it, but of a sudden my soul was lifted up, and I saw the Blessed Virgin in glory. And when I understood that a woman was placed in such majesty and glory and dignity as she was, I was marvellously delighted; for to see her was joy unutterable. For the Blessed Virgin Mary stood praying for the human race, and I saw her in such shapeliness and power of humanity that I cannot express it. And at this I was ineffably delighted. And while I was thus gazing on her, of a sudden there appeared Jesus Christ sitting by her side in his glorified Humanity.

Angela of Foligno

Because of the unique, exalted and wonderful love that he has for this sweet maiden, his blessed Mother, Our Lady St Mary, he showed her bliss and her joy through this sweet word, as if he said: 'Would you like to see how I love her so that you can rejoice with me in the love that I have for her and she for me?'

And also to understand this sweet word better, our good Lord speaks in love to all people who shall be saved, as if they were one single person. By this he seems to say: 'Do you want to see in her how much you are loved? It is for love of you that I created her so exalted, so noble, so worthy, and this pleases me. And I wish too that you be pleased with it.' For after himself she is the most blissful sight. But here I was taught that I should not long to see her physical presence whilst I am here on earth, but rather to seek the virtues of her blessed soul: her truth, her wisdom, her love, through which I will know myself and reverently fear God.

And when our good Lord had shown me this and said this word: 'Do you want to see her?' I answered and said: 'Yes, good Lord, thanks be to you, good Lord, if this be your will.' I said this prayer many times and I expected to see her in bodily likeness, but I did not see her so. And Jesus showed me in this word a spiritual sight of her.

And just as I had seen her before, little and simple, so he showed her to me now exalted, noble and glorious, and more pleasing to him than all creatures. And so he wants it to be known that all who take delight in him should also take delight in her, and rejoice in the delight that he has in her and she in him.

Julian of Norwich

Let the entire body of the faithful pour forth persevering prayer to the Mother of God and Mother of all people. Let them implore that she who aided the beginnings of the Church by her prayers may now, exalted as she is in heaven above all the saints and angels, intercede with her Son in the fellowship of all the saints. May she do so until all the peoples of the human family, whether they are honoured with the name of Christian or whether they still do not know their Saviour, are happily gathered together in peace and harmony into the one People of God, for the glory of the Most Holy and Undivided Trinity.

Vatican Council II

Hail, holy Queen, Mother of Mercy,
Hail, our life, our sweetness and our hope.
To you do we cry, poor banished children of Eve,
to you do we send up our sighs, mourning and
    weeping in this vale of tears.
Turn then, most gracious advocate, your eyes of
    mercy towards us;
and after this our exile,
show unto us the blessed fruit of your womb, Jesus.
O clement, O loving, O sweet Virgin Mary.

Hermann Contractus, 1054

Queen art thou of the shining angels,
Queen art thou of the happy saints,
Mother and Queen of exiled children,
Send us help when our courage faints.
Spotless Mother and Queen Divine,
All the love of our hearts is thine.
What shall we call thee, O beautiful Mother?
Lily of Israel, Rose without thorn,
Joy to thee, praise to thee, love to thee, thanks to thee,
Light of thy people, sweet Star of the morn.

S.N.D.

The Queenship of Mary

Hail Queen of heaven; hail mistress of the angels;
hail root of Jesse; hail the gate through which the
   Light rose over the earth.
Rejoice Virgin most renowned and of unsurpassed
   beauty.
Farewell, Lady most comely.
Prevail upon Christ to pity us.

Antiphon of the Virgin

No eye hath seen what joys the saints obtain,
No ear hath heard what comforts are possessed;
No heart can think in what delight they reign,
Nor pen express their happy port of rest,
Where pleasure flows, and grief is never seen,
Where good abounds and ill is banished clean.

Those sacred Saints remain in perfect peace,
Which Christ confessed, and walkèd in his ways,
They shine in bliss, which now can never cease,
And to his name do sing eternal praise:
Before his throne in white they ever stand,
And carry palms of triumph in their hand.

Above them all the Virgin hath a place,
Which caused the world with comfort to abound;
The beams do shine in her unspotted face,
And with the stars her head is richly crowned:
In glory she all creatures passeth far,
The moon her shoes, the sun her garments are.

St Philip Howard, 1595

Today we would linger
in your presence, O Sovereign!
I say again: Sovereign Virgin Mother of God,
and let us bind our souls,
as to a steadfast and immovable anchor,
to the hope that you are for us.
Let us dedicate to you our spirit and soul,
our body and our whole person.
We wish to honour you, as far as we are able,
with psalms, hymns and spiritual songs,
since it is impossible for us to honour you
according to your worth.
If, as a sign of the sacred word,
the honour which is offered to the servants
bears witness to the love towards our mutual Lord,
can we not pledge ourselves
to render honour to you, Mother of the Lord?
Ought we not pledge ourselves in every way?
Is it not desirable in our every breath,
from the very moment he gave us life,
in such a way that we demonstrate
our love for the Lord?
What am I saying, for the Lord?
In reality, for those who piously honour your memory
the precious gift of your memory is sufficient;
it becomes the highest expression of everlasting joy.
Does not this joy, these gifts,
fill the one whose soul has become
the dwelling for your sacred memory?

St John Damascene

Almighty God and Father,
you have given us Mary, the Mother of your Son,
to be our Mother and Queen.
Grant that, supported by her prayers,
we may come to the kingdom of heaven
and to the glory destined for your children.

Roman Missal

September 8

The Nativity of Mary

The Nativity of Mary has been observed in the Western Church since the eighth century and is primarily a feast of preparation for the Messiah.

Every child must have a mother, and we remember this every Christmas when we think of the birth of Jesus. But every mother was also once a child new-born herself. As Solomon says, no one has any other entrance into the world; everyone arrives naked and small and crying. There is not one of us who was not helpless, dependent and weak in infancy, relying upon a mother, or mother-substitute, to care for and nurture us. We share a common human condition whoever we are.

To outward eyes, emerging from the womb we may have looked just like any other baby. To our mother we appeared entirely special and beautiful. That is why families like to celebrate birthdays. It is as if we are telling those who are close to us that we are glad they are alive. That life for us would not be the same if they were not here. That their presence enriches the whole group.

What Mary looked like as a child we have no means of knowing, though we like to think that her inward beauty must have been reflected in her outward appearance. But when she was actually born she must have looked like any other infant, red and wrinkled and wizened, as she was taken from her mother to be washed and swaddled.

Jewish women of that time tended to squat or make use of a birthstool during labour; thus the emerging child followed the force of gravity and the birth would be easier. Men were totally excluded from witnessing this process, which was considered an affair for women only. There would be a midwife, maybe other women of the family, and the mother's mother looking on anxiously in the knowledge that labour could be dangerous and life-threatening. Jacob's beloved Rachel had died after a specially difficult confinement, and right through until quite modern times many men were married more than once through losing a wife in childbed. Jesus speaks of the pain a woman suffers during labour, followed by the joy, which makes her able to forget what went before. The ancient world was especially aware of what a child owed its mother for the gift of life, and enjoined reverence and obedience as a form of gratitude.

We know nothing of the circumstances of Mary's birth and parentage. Was her grandmother at the scene to advise her mother? Was there some disappointment that the infant was not a boy? The latter seems unlikely in that Mary, in view of her destiny, would be provided by God with parents who cherished and affirmed her, though at the time they would be quite unaware of her future role in salvation history.

To celebrate Mary's birthday is a way to thank God for her life. It is a day, too, to thank God for our own life, for the gift that we so often take for granted. Every baby is a sign of hope, a new beginning, a new attempt to embody the mystery of being. Reverence for life then is so important in our world, which is characterized by a 'throw-away' culture. Mary in her infancy, like all infants, has nothing to commend her except her precious existence.

To celebrate her birthday is to acknowledge the mystery of every child born into the world, and to offer a welcome.

* * *

Let your father and mother be glad;
and let her who bore you rejoice.

Proverbs 23:25

For it was you who formed my inmost parts;
you knit me together in my mother's womb.
I praise you, for I am fearfully and wonderfully made.
Wonderful are your works;
that I know very well.
My frame was not hidden from you,
when I was being made in secret,
intricately woven in the depths of the earth.
Your eyes beheld my unformed substance.
In your book were written all the days that were
    formed for me,
when none of them as yet existed.

Psalm 139:13–16

How beautiful you are, my love,
how very beautiful!
Your eyes are doves behind your veil.
You are altogether beautiful, my love;
there is no flaw in you.
Come with me from Lebanon, my bride,
come with me from Lebanon.
A garden locked is my sister, my bride,
a garden locked, a fountain sealed.
A garden fountain, a well of living water,
and flowing streams from Lebanon.

Song of Songs 4:1,7–8,12,15

The praise of true beauty belongs to the mind rather than the body. Yet in a certain way it belongs to the body as well, for it often happens that what a chaste heart conceives inwardly is manifested outwardly and becomingly through the agency of the body. But whatever is not born from purity of heart shows its impurity, since all the glory of the king's daughter comes from within. Yet not all her glory remains within! It often comes forth from her inmost parts and glorifies outwardly the King of Glory who is in heaven.

Baldwin of Ford, 1190

The Patriarch Abraham loved his son, Isaac, from the moment God promised him that he was to have a son. But with greater love did Almighty God himself love you, most blessed Virgin Mary, before anything was created, for he knew throughout eternity that you would be born to give him great joy . . .

Mary, daughter of Joachim, was a vessel closed and yet not closed. She was closed to the devil but not to God; for her heart was closed to all temptation. Instead the stream of my spirit flowed into her heart and filled her with special grace.

Secondly, Mary, the Mother of my Son, was a vessel small yet not small. Small and modest in her humble and insignificant position, great and not small in her love for the Deity.

Thirdly, Mary was a vessel empty yet not empty; empty of all worldliness and sin, yet not empty but filled with heavenly joy and virtue.

Fourthly, Mary was a vessel shining yet not shining. Shining, for every soul is created beautiful by me, and

171

Mary's soul grew to the perfection of light so that my Son could dwell in her soul over whose beauty heaven and earth rejoiced. But this vessel did not shine among humans for she despised earthly honour and riches.

Fifthly, Mary was a vessel chaste and yet not chaste, for she was fair throughout and in her there was not so much impurity as could be placed on the point of a needle; and yet not chaste for she was of Adam's race and born of sinners, although begotten without sin in order that she might bear my Son without sin.

Therefore, whoever comes to the place where Mary was born and nurtured shall not only be purified but even become a vessel for my grace.

St Bridget of Sweden

Your birth, O Mother of God, declared joy to all the
    universe:
for from you arose the Sun of Righteousness, Christ
    our Lord,
who broke the curse and gave the blessing,
who abolished death and bestowed on us the life
    which is eternal.
Joachim and Anne were freed from the reproach of
    childlessness,
and Adam and Eve from corruption and death
at your holy birth, O Virgin most pure.
Your birth is celebrated by the people also,
who are redeemed from the guilt of transgressions:
they sing to you –
The barren has given birth to the Mother of God
who nurtures our life.

Orthodox Liturgy

In Christ there was no thorn of sin
to turn into flower;
since he was the flower
born not of a thorn, but of a branch,
as the prophet said: 'He will come forth from a
    branch
of the stem of Jesse
and a flower will sprout from its roots.'
The branch was Mary,
tender, sincere and virgin
who bore Christ like a flower
through the integrity of her body.

Maximus of Turin,
Fourth–Fifth centuries

Our Lady's Nativity

Joy in the rising of our orient star
That shall bring forth that Sun that lent her light;
Joy in the peace that shall conclude our war,
And soon rebate the edge of Satan's spite;
Lode-star of all engulf'd in worldly waves,
The card and compass that from shipwreck saves.

The patriarchs and prophets were the flowers
Which time by course of ages did distill,
And culled into this little cloud the showers
Whose gracious drops the world with joy shall fill;
Whose moisture suppleth every soul with grace,
And bringeth life to Adam's dying race.

For God, on earth, she is the royal throne,
The chosen cloth to make his mortal weede;
The quarry to cut out our Corner stone,

Soil full of fruit, yet free from mortal seed;
For heavenly flower she is the Jesse rod,
The child of man, the parent of a God.

St Robert Southwell

Gentlest of all virgins,
that our love be faithful
keep us from all evil
gentle, strong and grateful.

Guard us through life's dangers
never turn and leave us,
may our hope find harbour
in the calm of Jesus.

Ave Maris Stella
(Trans. R. Wright)

According to the hymn we sing at Vespers on all her feasts, Mary is distinguished by her gentleness among women – among so many virgins and mothers on whom God has bestowed the grace of gentleness, yet whose very gentleness is at the same time their power and their strength. But all that is both virginal and maternal Mary, the second and spiritual Eve, possesses to an exceptional degree.

We are told that gentleness is the summing up of all the Christian virtues: it consists above all of patience and kindness; of respect and love for souls, indeed for all animate beings; since one who is gentle is gentle towards all living things.

Gentleness is the quality of a forgiving and merciful soul ... Mary had no need to condemn the world; it was the world that broke its strength against her graciousness.

A Carthusian

The Nativity of Mary

Blessed was the day
and welcome was the hour
whereon God's Virgin Mother
was brought forth.

For of that birth
Isaiah spoke
and said in prophecy
that a noble tree would spring
out of the root of Jesse,
and that this tree a bloom would bear
on which the Holy Spirit
of God himself would rest.

Blessed was the day
and welcome was the hour
whereon God's Virgin Mother
was brought forth.

King Alfonsus of Castile,
Thirteenth century

Who is this cometh over the mountains
Fair and sweet as the morning light,
Shedding holy and beautiful radiance
O'er the earth that was wrapt in night?
Now the dayspring indeed is nigh,
The morning star hath risen on high.
How shall we praise thee, O beautiful Mother?
How shall we greet thee newly born?
Joy to thee, praise to thee, love to thee, thanks to
    thee,
Hail to thy rising sweet Star of the Morn.

Wild and waste lay our desolate garden,
Stripped of blossom and leaf and fruit,
Lo, at last, in the golden autumn
Sprang the Lily from Jesse's root.
Hope and beauty came back to earth
Once again in Our Lady's birth.
How shall we welcome thee, beautiful Mother . . .

Spotless daughter of God the Father,
Future Mother of God the Son,
Fairest Bride of the Holy Spirit,
Beautiful Shrine of the Three-in-One:
O we thank him that he has given
So dear a Queen unto earth and heaven.
How shall we welcome thee, beautiful Mother . . .

S.N.D.

September 15

Our Lady of Sorrows

The feast of Our Lady of Sorrows follows on the feast of
the Exaltation of the Cross kept on 14 September. The
Exaltation of the Cross was established to commemorate
St Helena's finding of the true Cross in Jerusalem, and later
its recovery from the Persians by the Emperor Heraclitus
in 628. It is a feast of splendour and imperial magnificence,
the Cross being hailed as the sign of salvation, the instrument of our redemption. Christ rules from the Cross,
bejewelling it with drops of his blood. It is the 'noble tree'
bearing fruit like no other. This is not the time to consider
the pain of Christ but his victory over suffering and death.

> Tree of light! whose branches shine
> With purple royal and divine;
> Elect on whose triumphal breast
> Those holy limbs should find their rest!

> Vespers Hymn

The first representations of the crucified Saviour depict him
as a king in glory, not a man dying in agony.

With the Middle Ages and the increase of devotion to
the human Christ, Jesus of Nazareth, there arose a deeper
appreciation of his physical sufferings and the concomitant
suffering of the Mother who watched him die. Simeon's
prophecy that a sword would pierce her heart was inter-

preted as being fulfilled in Mary's presence on Calvary, when she had to watch helplessly as her Son hung in agony. The remembrance of the Mother of Sorrows brings our thoughts back from the glory underlying the Cross to the human suffering involved. To suffer in union with Christ, to remain near the Cross with him, is our part in redemption. In this Mary is our model, she is the compassionate one.

Passion always has its roots in the body. To become fully human we have to search the depths of our own humanity, so that the seed of compassion, a pure flame of love, can be kindled in us, body and soul.

The Letter to the Hebrews says that Jesus was tempted in all things as we are, yet did not sin. Only of one other person could that be said – Mary. Surely she, the new Eve, was able to grasp silently and sensitively, as none other, something of the inner reality that comprised the Passion of her Son. How seldom we consider what it must have meant experientially for Mary to sound out her own humanity, face her womanhood in those reaches where she was in touch with elemental forces beyond her conscious control: the very springs of life and love within her, and the overpowering strength of the maternal instinct to shield her offspring from pain.

Somehow we seem to have imbibed an erroneous idea that, while Jesus was tempted, temptation would not be 'fitting' for his Mother. It brings her closer to us if we realize that Mary too would have had to wrestle with temptation – maybe with her possessiveness, over-dependency, self-pity, or even with the very natural desire for more children.

Mary had to face life, as we all do, not in a disembodied, 'pious' way, but courageously, in all her vulnerable humanness. It is only when we have touched the depths of our weakness that we can experience the power of grace; for grace must be inserted in the core of our existence or it has no lasting power to transform us – and Mary is grace-filled as is no other.

Mary knew experientially on Calvary (which must have marked the key point of her temptation to despair as she saw her Son abandoned), that if only she could reach out and hold on, trusting that God would accomplish his will beyond all human reckoning, victory would come from this terrible anguish.

The Mother of Sorrows is the woman who stayed closest to the Lord, even when she did not understand; even when all seemed lost. How many mothers today see a child suffer and wish they could take the child's place. And yet they must remain doing nothing except just 'being there'. Often that is all *we* can do for the Lord. It is the only proof of love we can give. And it is this which breaks open our hearts to understand the pain of others and stay close.

* * *

She weeps bitterly in the night, with tears on her
  cheeks;
among all her lovers she has no one to comfort her;
all her friends have dealt treacherously with her,
they have become her enemies.
Is it nothing to you all who pass by?
Look and see if there is any sorrow like my sorrow,
which was brought upon me, which the Lord inflicted
on the day of his fierce anger.
Cry aloud to the Lord! O wall of daughter Zion!
Let tears stream down like a torrent day and night!
Give yourself no rest, your eyes no respite.

Lamentations 1:2,12; 2:18

179

Meanwhile, standing near the cross of Jesus were his mother, and his mother's sister, Mary the wife of Clopas, and Mary Magdalene. When Jesus saw his mother and the disciple whom he loved standing beside her, he said to his mother, 'Woman, here is your son.' Then he said to the disciple, 'Here is your mother.' And from that hour the disciple took her into his own home.

John 19:25–27

The Queen of Virgins is the Queen of Martyrs too, but it was within her heart that the sword transpierced her, for with her everything took place within her soul. Oh, how beautiful she is in a majesty both strong and sweet, for she has learned from the Word himself how they should suffer who are chosen as victims by the Father; those whom he has elected as associates in the great work of redemption; 'those whom he foreknew he also predestined to be made conformable to his Son,' crucified by love. She is there at the foot of the Cross, standing in her strength and courage, and my Master says to me: '*Ecce Mater tua.*' He gives her to me for my Mother! And now that he has returned to the Father, he has put me in his place on the Cross, so that I may 'fill up those things that are wanting in the sufferings of Christ for his Body which is the Church.' Mary is there still, to teach me to suffer as he did, to tell me, to make me hear those last outpourings of his soul, which only his Mother could catch.

Elizabeth of the Trinity

Mary's heart and love have been shaped by sorrow. Her love therefore is utterly compassionate. During the whole of her life on earth – above all when she stood at the foot of the Cross – Mary's soul was pierced and wounded by that sorrowful sword, her compassion for the Being most dear to her. None has known as she has known that torture of martyrdom which compassion for her agonizing Son inflicted upon her. There could be no more moving reason than this why Mary's love is a profoundly compassionate love. Were the Virgin herself not our Mother, she, the Queen of Martyrs, would indeed be the ideal soul to which we could confide all our sufferings and all our needs.

Paul de Jaegher

O holy Mary, afflicted Mother, tell me somewhat of the Passion of the blessed Son of God, because you have seen more of the Passion than any other saint, by reason of the zeal which you had continually for him who was your Love. For you saw him with the eyes of your body and the eyes of your soul. You gazed upon him most earnestly because you loved him exceedingly ... And my soul perceived that the Passion of Christ was so great that although holy Mary saw more than any other saint, yet in many ways I understand that in nowise could she express it, nor any other saint.

Angela of Foligno

Here I saw something of the compassion of Our Lady St Mary, for Christ and she were so one in love that the greatness of her love was the cause of the greatness of her pain. In this I saw the substance of natural love, developed by grace, which his creatures have for him.

This love was most supremely and surpassingly shown in his sweet Mother. For as much as she loved him more than all others, her pain surpassed all others. For always the higher, the stronger, the sweeter the love is, the greater is the sorrow of one who sees the body of a beloved suffer. So all his disciples and all his true lovers suffered far more when he suffered than when they themselves did. I am sure, from the way I feel myself, that the very least of them loved him so much more than they loved themselves that I am unable to put it into words.

Julian of Norwich

Come to me, loving Mary, that I may keen with you your very dear one. Alas that your Son should go to the Cross, he who was a great diadem, a beautiful hero.

That with you I may beat my two hands for the captivity of your beautiful Son: your womb has conceived Jesus – it has not marred your virginity . . .

Your people seized your Son, Mary; they flogged him. There struck him the green reed and fists across ruddy cheeks.

When every outrage was committed against him, when capture was completed, he took his Cross upon his back – he did not cease being beaten.

When his Cross was placed between the two crosses of the condemned ones he was raised (alas!) upon the Cross; it was very pitiful.

A crown of thorns was placed (this was severe excess) about his beautiful head; nails were driven through his feet, others through his hands.

A purple cloak was put about the King by the ignoble assembly; in mockery that was put about him, not from a desire to cover him.

The Son of God the Father! A reed was put in his hand at the end; it was said, clearly to mock him, that he was King of the Jews.

They tore from him his pure raiment; beautiful was the body that they stripped; lots were cast without any deception to see who might take his blessed spoils.

When they thought thus that Jesus could be approached, Longinus then came to slay him with the spear.

The King of the seven holy heavens, when his heart was pierced, wine spilled upon the pathways, the blood of Christ flowing through his gleaming sides.

Beautiful maiden, were a hundred tongues to speak of it they could not recount the extent of your Son's power: the repetition would not achieve completeness.

He is the true priest according to the order of Melchisedech; it is that God, the Father, created a time before the morning star.

It is your Son's body that comes to us when we go to the Sacrament; the pure wine has been transmuted for us into the blood of the Son of the King.

Blathmac (Irish, *c.*700)

What mist hath dimmed that glorious face?
What seas of grief my sun doth toss?
The golden rays of heavenly grace
lie now eclipsèd on the cross.

Jesus! my Love, my Son, my God,
behold thy mother washed in tears;
Thy bloody wounds be made a rod
to chasten these my latter years.

Thou messenger that didst impart
his first descent into my womb,
Come help me now to cleave my heart,
that I may there my Son intomb.

Ye angels all, that present were,
to show his birth in harmony;
Why are you not now ready here,
to make a mourning symphony?

But wail, my soul, thy comfort dies,
my woeful womb lament thy fruit;
My heart, give tears unto my eyes,
let sorrow string my heavy lute.

St Robert Southwell

God in whom all grace doth dwell!
Grant us grace to ponder well
On the Virgin's dolours seven,
On the wounds to Jesus given.

May the tears which Mary poured
Grant us pardon of the Lord!
Tears excelling in their worth
All the penances of earth.

May the contemplation sore
Of the wounds which Jesus bore,
Source to us of blessings be
Through a long eternity.

Callisto Palunabella,
Eighteenth century

Mother, fount whence love flows truest,
Let me know the pain thou knewest,
Let me weep as thou hast wept;
Love divine within me burning,
That diviner love returning,
May thy Son this heart accept.

Jacopone da Todi, 1306

September 24

Our Lady of Ransom – Our Lady of Mercy

The title of Our Lady of Ransom arose from an apparition of Our Lady to St Peter Nolasco on 1 August 1233 in Barcelona Cathedral, where the original Ransom Shrine is to be found. The Blessed Virgin reputedly showed St Peter a white tunic with a red and blue cross that was to be the habit of a new Order, named the Mercedenarian Friars, who would pray and collect alms for the ransoming of Christian captives held by the Moors. King James of Aragon, in whose kingdom the Moors were especially active, gave his consent, and St Peter, together with St Raymond of Pennafort, laid the foundation of the Ransomers.

This was no empty vocation, because the friars promised to offer themselves as ransom personally if required to do so. When it is remembered that, among others, St Vincent de Paul and Fr Jerome Gracian, friend of St Teresa of Avila, spent time in Moorish captivity, it becomes obvious that this apostolate was a costly one. Of course, captivity worked both ways, and captured Moors became the slaves of Christian families in their turn.

The dictionary defines 'ransom' as: 'to buy back, to liberate for a considerable sum of money, redeem, purchase freedom, atone for, expiate.' In the Old Testament God himself is called the Redeemer of his people, and in the New Testament the title is passed to Jesus as the Christ. Taking our sins on himself, Jesus offers himself to the Father on our behalf, and thus obtains for us the freedom of the children of God.

Even today, to ransom someone is no light matter. A family may have to sell or mortgage all they have in order to pay kidnappers to release one of their number. But love motivates them. For love they are willing to give all they have, and think nothing of the loss.

The 'ransoming' instituted by Peter Nolasco arose from a specific historical situation, but now the title is extended to *all* works of mercy connected with the slavery of disease, ignorance, hunger, deprivation in all its forms. This feast is the titular of the Sisters of Mercy throughout the world, as well as a feast particularly kept in England, owing to the desire of many to sacrifice themselves in order to bring England back to the Catholic faith.

Mary is thought of as the model and inspiration of the merciful – those who offer their lives (in one way or another) for their fellow men and women, just as she did because of her love for, and union with, the mission of her Son.

At the heart of the mystery of mercy lies a passion for souls and a deep sense of the Church. We are linked together in Christ: 'Who is suffering and I do not grieve?' says St Paul. The books of contemporaries like Bonhoeffer and Richard Wurmbrandt show how much the persecuted Church relies on prayer and practical help from those who enjoy their freedom. 'I believe I owe it to the prayers of others, both known and unknown, that I have so often been preserved in safety,' Bonhoeffer wrote from his prison cell.

Those who love the Church cultivate a sense of solidarity, of caring for one another, of passing on what they consider valuable. Also mercy, spiritual or temporal, is what touches hearts because mercy *costs* in effort, time, self-giving. Mercy takes us away from constant preoccupation with ourselves, and reminds us of the truth that we are part of the whole mystical body of Christ, and indeed part of all humanity.

The witness of our lives is what counts. To cultivate an attitude of mercy and self-giving because we belong together in the merciful Christ is a powerful motive for prayer and sacrifice.

Many early pictures of Our Lady of Mercy show her with all kinds of people held safely sheltered within her spread mantle. Because she is Mother she enfolds all of us who are poor and needy in order to present us to the Son she loves. 'Blessed are the merciful, for they shall have mercy shown to them.'

* * *

> *Bless the Lord, O my soul,*
> *and all that is within me, bless his holy name.*
> *Bless the Lord, O my soul,*
> *and do not forget all his benefits –*
> *who forgives all your iniquity,*
> *who heals all your diseases,*
> *who redeems your life from the Pit,*
> *who crowns you with steadfast love and mercy.*

> *Psalm 103:1–4*

On the third day there was a wedding in Cana of Galilee, and the mother of Jesus was there. Jesus and his disciples had also been invited to the wedding.

Our Lady of Ransom – Our Lady of Mercy

When the wine gave out, the mother of Jesus said to him, 'They have no wine.' And Jesus said to her, 'Woman, what concern is that to you and to me? My hour has not yet come.' His mother said to the servants, 'Do whatever he tells you.'

John 2:1–5

O how humbly has God shown his compassion in this world through the Virgin Mary who can properly be called the Tree of Life! If people desire to refresh themselves with the fruit of this tree, which is Christ, they must first with all their might strive to bend the branches of the tree, that is to say, to venerate God's Mother devoutly, in the same way as did the angel at the Annunciation, and – so that every sin may be avoided – strengthen their resolution and wisely direct all their words and deeds towards the glory of God. For then the Virgin will willingly bend down to them and offer her help in obtaining the fruit of the Tree of Life, namely Christ's most holy body which among you is consecrated by human hands and which is nourishment and life for you, sinners here on earth, and for angels in heaven.

St Bridget of Sweden

O glorious Queen of Heaven, Virgin Mary!
Turn to me the eyes of your mercy.
Receive me under your protection,
for my comfort and hope are in you.
Oh, how many had already abandoned God,
had given up all hope of gaining heaven,
had cast themselves headlong into the depths of
    despair,

and were miserably separated from God;
and yet by leaning on you and flying to you
they have been most kindly kept by you,
until by your prayers
they have been restored at last to God's grace!
Was there ever a sinner so great,
so tightly bound with the chains of iniquity,
that, remembering you, was not inspired with fresh
    courage and hope?
Yes, truly you are the chosen and most faithful
    comforter of sinners.
Therefore most tender mother,
mistress of heaven and earth arise!
Arise and show yourself our advocate and peacemaker
    with your sweet Son,
that he as a favour may blot out our sins
and bring us to life everlasting.

Bl. Henry Suso

I say that we are wound
With mercy round and round
As if with air: the same
Is Mary, more by name,
She, wild web, wondrous robe,
Mantles the guilty globe.
Since God has let dispense
Her prayers His providence.
Nay, more than almoner,
The sweet alms' self is her
And men are meant to share
Her life as life does air.

Gerard Manley Hopkins

Mary, I beg you, by that grace
through which the Lord is with you
and you willed to be with him,
let your mercy be with me.
Let love for you always be with me,
and the care of me always be with you.
Let the cry of my need, as long as it persists, be with
    you,
and the care of your goodness, as long as I need it, be
    with me.
Let joy in your blessedness be always with me.
and compassion for my wretchedness, where I need it,
    be with you.

St Anselm, 1109

Holy Mary, succour the wretched,
help the disheartened,
put new heart into the feeble.
Pray for the people,
intercede for the clergy,
pray for all women dedicated to God.
May all those who honour your memory
experience your generous help.
You attend promptly to the voices of those who pray
    to you
and satisfy the desire of each one.
Let your undertaking be diligent intercession
for the people of God.
For you merited, O blessed one,
to bear the ransom of the world,
he who lives and reigns for ever and ever. Amen.

Fulbert of Chartres, 1028

Times and seasons change, centuries and ages pass;
you seem above them, Lord, untouched, unmoved.
But your Son entered in, born of a woman,
crushed and crucified, to ransom us.
Will you be deaf to our cries?
Can you ignore the appeals
of the creatures your Son embraced?
Can you refuse the prayer of Mary, his Mother?
Let us know the freedom of your Kingdom
where you live with your Son
and with the Holy Spirit,
one infinite Freedom
for ever and ever.

Roman Missal

Maiden, yet a Mother,
Daughter of thy Son,
High beyond all other –
Lowlier is none;
Thou the consummation
Planned by God's decree,
When our lost creation
Nobler rose in thee!

Thus his place preparèd,
He who all things made
'Mid his creatures tarried,
In thy bosom laid;
There his love he nourished –
Warmth that gave increase
To the Root whence flourished
Our eternal peace.

Nor alone thou hearest
When thy name we hail;
Often thou art nearest
When our voices fail;
Mirrored in thy fashion
All creation's good,
Mercy, might, compassion
Grace thy womanhood.

Dante Alighieri, 1321
(Trans. R. Knox)

October 7

Our Lady of the Rosary

One of the most famous pictures by the artist Cezanne, painted around 1898, shows an old woman from an asylum sitting with bent head. Her weathered face and emphatic pose give the impression of great solidity. Her hands hold a rosary, and she clasps the beads as if giving herself to prayer with the simplicity of long habit. She embodies in her quiet concentration the part the rosary has played in the lives of numerous men and women. When one can do nothing else one can at least hold the beads; they can be passed through the fingers in an intentional rhythm of constant prayer, and the Hail Marys flow like limpid water, whether spoken aloud or in silence. It is the prayer of mothers and children, of sailors at sea, of philosophers and artists. The rosary is always there to turn to when words fail and meditation dries up. For many the rosary is the last prayer they hear as they lie dying, and the familiar beads will be entwined around their fingers as they are placed in the coffin.

There is then a distinction to be made between today's feast as an historical event and the rosary as a prayer form. The feast itself was introduced to commemorate the victory of the Christian forces over the Turks at the battle of Lepanto on 7 October 1571; a victory that was considered an answer to prayer, as the Turkish forces were superior in every way. But the emphasis of the feast now is on the rosary as a Marian devotion which brings us close to Jesus through pondering his life, Passion and Resurrection in company with his Mother.

The rosary as we know it now seems to have evolved out of the use of beads for praying, such as was common practice among the Muslims, and was possibly a custom brought back to Europe and adapted for Christian use at the time of the Crusades. The Dominican Order was especially active in promoting the rosary, which became known as Our Lady's Psalter, the 150 Hail Marys substituting for the 150 psalms of the Divine Office at a time when many were unable to read.

The counting of the Ave Marias by means of beads was a practical aid in tallying 150 without having to concentrate on the mathematics involved. The first Lady Godiva, who died in 1075, left a string of precious stones in the form of a 'prayer counter' to be hung round the neck of the statue of Our Lady in the monastery she had helped to found at Coventry.

The practice of meditating on a mystery of the life of Jesus and/or Mary for the space of a *Pater noster*, 10 *Ave*s and a *Gloria*, gave the rosary a specific focus. It could be used as a method of contemplation, of praying vocally, or a combination of the two. It did not require erudition or great spiritual gifts. The rosary was, and is, for everyone.

By devoting a certain amount of time, measured out by the recitation of set prayers, a prayer space is offered to God as the beads pass through the fingers. The comfort of holding something, the rhythm of the words, the pondering on the mysteries, and the gentle rise and fall of the breath, make the rosary ideal for silent or communal recitation.

The word 'rosary' was obviously derived from the flower of that name, the rose being considered the most beautiful and fragrant bloom of medieval times. The custom of weaving roses into garlands of honour at special celebrations like weddings made this 'spiritual garland' an ideal gift for Mary that seemed specially appropriate. Also the garden is a place of labour as well as relaxation. The saying of the beads can be a work of love when we have determined to give this time to God and do not feel like doing so. The very fact of sitting there and 'telling [tallying] the beads' is a token of intent.

In recent years the rosary has experienced a revival in popularity through introducing new ways of approaching it. Sometimes relevant passages from Scripture are inserted between the *Ave*s, or at the end of a decade. Sometimes the prayers used are scriptural mantras linked to the mysteries and repeated on every bead. Other people like to choose their own combination of mysteries to meditate on, rather than keeping to the traditional fifteen.

All in all, the rosary seems set to remain a popular prayer for many years to come. It is a way of honouring Mary by meditating with her on her Son's life, death and Resurrection. It involves senses, mind and spirit. It is a prayer for everyone, young and old, and it demonstrates that contemplation is available to all and as simple as fingering lovingly a string of beads!

* * *

O Lord, my heart is not lifted up,
my eyes are not raised too high;
I do not occupy myself with things
too great and marvellous for me.
But I have calmed and quieted my soul,
like a weaned child with its mother;
my soul is like the weaned child that is with me.
O Israel, hope in the Lord
from this time on and for evermore.

Psalm 131:1–3

He looked up and saw rich people putting their gifts into the treasury; he also saw a poor widow put in two small copper coins. He said, 'Truly I tell you, this poor widow has put in more than all of them; for all of them have contributed out of their abundance, but she out of her poverty has put in all she had to live on.'

Luke 21:1–4

Ask and it will be given you; search and you will find; knock, and the door will be opened for you.

For everyone who asks, receives, and everyone who searches, finds, and for everyone who knocks, the door will be opened.

Luke 11:9–10

The gladness of thy motherhood,
The anguish of thy suffering,
The glory now that crowns thy brow,
O Virgin Mother, we would sing.

Hail, blessed Mother, full of joy
In thy consent, thy visit too:
Joy in the birth of Christ on earth,
Joy in him lost, and found anew.

Hail, sorrowing in his agony –
The blows, the thorns that pierced his brow;
The heavy wood, the shameful Rood –
Yea! Queen and chief of martyrs thou.

Hail in the triumph of thy Son,
The quickening flames of Pentecost;
Shining a Queen in light serene,
When all the world is tempest-tost.

O come, ye nations, roses bring,
Culled from these mysteries divine,
And for the Mother of your King
With loving hands your chaplets twine.

We lay our homage at thy feet,
Lord Jesus, thou the Virgin's Son,
With Father and with Paraclete
Reigning while endless ages run.

Augustine Rucchini OP,
Eighteenth century

The Rosary consists of holy words, and the Hail Mary takes precedence over all. Its first part is derived from the New Testament. It begins with the message of the angel in Nazareth, 'Hail, full of grace, the Lord is with thee.' This is followed by the words with which Elizabeth greeted Mary when she crossed the mountains to visit her: 'Blessed art thou among women and blessed is the fruit of thy womb.' The second part is an ancient appeal for Mary's intercession . . . The Our Father the Lord himself gave us as the perfect model and substance of Christian prayer . . . The Creed forms the first expression of Christian conviction . . . The 'Glory be to the Father and to the Son and to the Holy Spirit' is the glorification of the triune God in its simplest form . . . Finally, with the sign of the Cross, with which the Rosary begins and ends – 'In the Name of the Father and of the Son and of the Holy Spirit' – Christians from remote antiquity have placed themselves under the name of God and the sign of redemption.

These words are recurrent. They create that open, moving world, transfused by energy and regulated by reason, in which the act of prayer takes place ... And when the words are those of Holy Scripture, they become an arch into the sacred room of revelation, in which the truth of the living God is made known to us.

Within this room built by the sacred Word, the figure of Mary appears as the immediate content of the Rosary prayer.

She has been dear to Christian hearts from the beginning. Already the disciples of Jesus surrounded her with special love and respect. One is conscious of this in following the occasional but quite numerous places in the Gospels and Acts that speak of her. The Christian people have always loved Mary with a love specially reserved for her, and it was not a good omen when Christians thought of severing their bond to Mary in order to honour the Son ...

It is Mary on whom the Rosary is centred in a focus ever new. This prayer means a lingering in the world of Mary, whose essence was Christ ...

If a person becomes very important to us, we are happy to meet someone who is attached to him. We see his image mirrored in another life and we see it anew. Our eyes meet two eyes that also love and see. They add their range of vision to ours, and our gaze may now go beyond the narrowness of our ego and embrace the beloved being, previously seen only from one side. The joys that the other person experienced, and also the pains he suffered, become as many strings whose vibrations draw from our hearts new notes, new understanding, and new responses ... Something of this sort, only on a higher plane, happens with the Rosary.

Romano Guardini

In the doorway of the low grey house,
built of stones as old as the Crusades,
a woman of Bruges
sits in the sunlight, among the flowers,
saying her Rosary.

The story of Mary is her own story,
and her son was her life's joy
and her life's sorrow;
and for ever
her son is her life's glory.

In a field in Flanders,
among the red poppies,
he is sleeping;
he will sleep soundly
until the day of resurrection.

She has still the patchwork quilt
made, when her hands were nimble,
for the wooden cot:
now he is sleeping, and each year
he has a new coverlet
of delicate young grass,
and at the end of his cot
a wooden cross.

The cradle of wood,
the wood of the cross;
from cradle to cross,
like a lullaby.

The story of the old woman of Bruges
is the world's story.
It is the story
of human joy and sorrow,

woven and interlaced,
like the blue and crimson threat
in woven cloth:
the story of birth and death,
of war and the rumours of war,
and of peace past understanding,
peace in the souls that live
in the life of Christ.

In the doorway in Bruges,
sitting among the flowers,
her mind like a velvet bee
droning over a rose,
taking the honey of comfort
out of the heart of Love,
the old woman is nodding
over her Rosary.

She has lived her meditation,
like the Mother of God,
living the life of Christ:
let her sleep in Christ's peace.

Caryll Houselander

Mary,
how many times have I found
when I have come to appeal to you,
that you have healed the aching wounds of my heart.

Guido Gezelle

O Mary, you are praying for us, you are always praying
for us. We know it, we feel it. Oh what joy and truth, what
sublime glory, in this heavenly and human interchange of

sentiments, words and actions, which the Rosary always brings us: the tempering of our human afflictions, the fore-taste of the peace that is not of this world, the hope of eternal life!

Pope John XXIII

November 21

The Presentation of Mary in the Temple

The feast of Mary's Presentation in the temple has been kept in the East since the eighth century. It seems to be associated with the basilica of St Mary the New in Jerusalem, which was dedicated on 21 November 543, and was probably an annual memorial kept in this particular church. Later it was celebrated throughout Jerusalem, and later still reached Constantinople and thence the West. In the West it has never attained the same prominence as in the East, although the seminarians of St Sulpice traditionally renew the promises of tonsure on 21 November and the Carmelites have celebrated it with particular solemnity also as a day of prayer for novices.

The story of the Presentation of Mary, as we have it now, is taken from the apocryphal Gospel of James which delights in imaginatively recounting the early years of the Mother of God. The author describes the grief of Joachim and Anne, Mary's parents, at their childlessness, and they promise that, if they are granted a child, she shall belong entirely to God. Shortly afterwards Anne conceives and in due course gives birth to an infant girl, Mary. In fulfilment of the promise, the child is taken to the temple at the age of three, where she is met by a procession of young girls with lighted torches. She joyfully runs up the steps of the sanctuary to be welcomed by the high priest. Mary remains in the holy of holies, being fed by an angel, until her betrothal to Joseph when she reaches the age of puberty.

This story is obviously derived from that of Samuel, whose mother, Hannah, prays for offspring, promising to dedicate the child to God in the event of her prayer being heard.

Excavations and the perusal of ancient texts alike all conspire to demonstrate that there is no historical foundation for thinking that there was a place in the temple precincts for girls to reside and be educated. This story is fiction, not fact.

So what can be garnered from this feast about Mary and about ourselves? Surely it is that every vocation takes time and careful preparation. In her childhood Mary is being prepared for her future task as Mother of God. She is the living holy of holies, the new temple, bearing Christ in her body, always listening to God in silent attentiveness.

Jesus promises that children are the ones who will enter the Kingdom of Heaven. We should never treat children's religious experience lightly. Their sense of God can be a precious gift, inciting us to wonder and prayer. Mary was always 'child' with God: absolute trust and love and humility. This feast symbolizes her wholehearted acceptance of God's call to her, and we do not know how young she was when she began to respond consciously to his love and his choice. St Thérèse could say that from the age of three she had never refused God anything. Three is not too young to be aware of the Divine presence, and vocation always implies God's choice coupled with human response. We are not dragooned into God's service like mindless robots.

I doubt Mary thought much of herself and her own perfection. She was too aware of life, and her need to be present to each moment, to consider what others thought of her, whether or not she was 'special'. Indeed I doubt she was even aware that she was different from others of her age and class. Certainly her preparation to be Mother of God had nothing to do with the perfect keeping of rules, being segregated in some kind of Jewish 'nunnery' or anything like that!

Mary's perfection consisted rather in having an 'attentive heart'. These early years are her 'desert experience', her years of silence before she emerges to utter her '*Fiat*' and then revert once more to the silence of Bethlehem and Nazareth. She renounces merely earthly things and centres herself on God from youth upwards. This does not imply a lack of reverence for creation; Judaism, as no other religion, is rooted in reverence for this world. But silence and attentiveness are practised in order to pass beyond exterior beauty and taste the kernel of Mystery.

The gift of self to God is not a once-for-all happening; it is a continuous process. Often we can discover its roots in our childhood, and that is where we have to return in meditation to recapture the wonder of life when it flowed freshly for us from the hand of God, and touched every aspect of the world around us.

So this feast of Mary's presentation is a feast of preparation. In it we remember those years during which she was silently being prepared for the mystery that would take place in her at Advent. And so the Marian year begins again . . .

* * *

Hannah said, 'For this child I prayed; and the Lord has granted me my petition. Therefore I have lent [this child] to the Lord; as long as [she] lives, [she] is given to the Lord.

1 Samuel 1:27–28 (adapted)

The Presentation of Mary in the Temple

How lovely is your dwelling place, O Lord of hosts!
My soul longs, indeed it faints
for the courts of the Lord;
my heart and my flesh sing for joy to the living God.
Even the sparrow finds a home,
and the swallow a nest for herself,
where she may lay her young,
at your altars, O Lord of hosts, my King and my
   God.
Happy are those who live in your house,
ever singing your praise.

Psalm 84:1–4

Do you not know that your body is a temple of the Holy
Spirit within you, which you have from God, and that you
are not your own? For you were bought with a price;
therefore glorify God in your body.

1 Corinthians 6:19–20

Today is the prelude of God's goodwill and the pre-heralding of our salvation. In the temple of God the Virgin plainly appeareth, and proclaimeth Christ to all. To her let us also cry out with a loud voice – Rejoice, O fulfilment of the Creator's dispensation. The most pure Temple of the Saviour, the highly precious Bridal Chamber, the Virgin, the holy Treasury of the glory of God, is today led into the house of the Lord, and bringeth with her the grace which is in the Divine Spirit. Of her the angels of God sing – This is the heavenly Tabernacle.

Orthodox Liturgy

This is that blessed Mary, pre-elect
God's virgin. Gone is a great while, and she
Dwelt young in Nazareth of Galilee.
Unto God's will she brought devout respect,
Profound simplicity of intellect,
And supreme patience. From her mother's knee
Faithful and hopeful; wise in charity;
Strong in grave peace; in pity circumspect.

So held she through her girlhood, as it were
An angel-watered lily, that near God
Grows and is quiet. Till, one dawn at home,
She woke in her white bed, and had no fear
At all – yet wept 'til sunshine, and felt awed:
Because the fullness of the time was come.

Dante Gabriel Rossetti

'If you knew the gift of God,' Christ said one evening to the Samaritan woman. Yet what is this gift of God, but himself? 'He came to his own and his own did not receive him,' declares the beloved disciple. To many a soul might John the Baptist still utter the reproach. 'There has stood one in the midst of you whom you knew not.' 'If only you knew the gift of God!'

There is one created being who did know the gift of God, who lost no particle of it; a creature so pure and luminous that she seemed to be the Light itself: a being whose life was so simple, so lost in God, that there is but little to say of it: the faithful Virgin who 'kept all these things in her heart.'

She was so lowly, so hidden in God in the seclusion of the temple, that she drew upon herself the complacent regard of the Holy Trinity: 'Because he has regarded the humility of his handmaiden; for behold from henceforth all generations shall call me blessed.' The Father, bending down to this lovely creature, so unaware of her own beauty, chose her for the Mother in time of him whose Father he is for all eternity. Then the Spirit of Love, who presides over all the works of God, overshadowed her; the Virgin uttered her *Fiat*: 'Behold the handmaid of the Lord; be it done to me according to your word,' and the greatest of all mysteries was accomplished. By the descent of the Word into her womb, Mary became God's own for ever and ever.

Elizabeth of the Trinity

Hail Mary, sweetest daughter of Anne!
Love attracts me to you anew.
How can I describe your decorous bearing?
And your dress?
And the beauty of your face?
And the prudent bearing in your prime of life?
Your dress was modest,
far removed from any extravagance,
your step is solemn, neither headlong nor flagging;
your conduct is thoughtful, lightened by youthful
    liveliness,
and greatest prudence towards others.
This was shown in the awe which surrounded you
at the unexpected meeting with the angel.
You were gentle and respectful towards your parents;
humble in spirit in the highest contemplation;
agreeable was the speech which came forth from your
    gentle soul.
In brief, naught else in you

is not the worthy dwelling place of God.
Rightly all generations call you blessed,
for you are the glory of the human race,
you are the pride of priests,
the hope of Christians,
the fruitful plant of virginity;
through you, in truth, the beauty of virginity is
  widespread.
Blessed are you among women
and blessed is the fruit of your womb.

St John Damascene

O Maiden most immaculate,
Make me to choose the better part,
And give my Lord, with love as great,
An undivided heart.

Would that my heart, dear Lord, were true,
Royal and undefiled and whole,
Like hers from whom thy sweet love took
The Blood to save my soul.

F. W. Faber

Sources and Acknowledgements

All Biblical quotations are from the NRSV. The New Revised Standard Version of the Bible, copyright 1989, Division of Christian Education of the National Council of the Churches of Christ in the United States of America, is published in London by HarperCollins Publishers.

With gratitude to the following publishers for permission to quote from copyright material: to Ave Maria Press for three passages from *Blessed art Thou* by R. Beyer; to Bear and Company USA for selections from *Meditations with Hildegard of Bingen*, trans. by G. Uhlen; to Paulist Press USA for passages from *The Tree of Life* by St Bonaventure, trans. E. Cousins; to Sheed and Ward for quotations from *The Reed of God* and *The Flowering Tree* by Caryll Houselander; to St Paul publishers for selections from *Sing the Joys of Mary, Hymns from the First Millennium*, trans. P. Jenkins..

Any copyrights that have been inadvertently overlooked will be remedied in any further editions of this book.

Aelred, St, *Letter to his Sister*, trans. G. Webb and A. Walker, Mowbray, 1957

Andersson, A., *St Bridget of Sweden*, CTS, 1980

Angela of Foligno, *Visions and Instructions*, trans. 'a Secular Priest', Richardson, 1871

Anselm, St, *Prayers and Meditations*, trans. B. Ward, Penguin, 1973

Asch, S., *Mary*, McDonald, 1950

Baldwin of Ford, *Spiritual Tractates Vol 1*, trans. D. Bell, Cistercian Publications, 1986

Berselli, C., and Gharig, G. (eds), *Sing the Joys of Mary – Hymns from the First Millennium*, trans. P. Jenkins, St Paul, 1980

Beyer, R., *Blessed art Thou*, Ave Maria Press, 1996

Blosius, L., *Comfort for the Fainthearted*, trans. B. Wilberforce, Burns, Oates and Washbourne, 1926

Bonaventure, St, *The Tree of Life*, trans. E. Cousins, Paulist, 1978

Carthusian, A, *The Prayer of Love and Silence*, DLT, 1962

Carthusian, A, *They Speak by Silences*, Longman's Green, 1955

Carthusian Monks, *Ancient Devotions to the Sacred Heart of Jesus*, Burns and Oates, 1926

Claudel, P., *Lord, Teach us to Pray*, Dobson, 1942

Damien, St Peter, *Selected Writings on the Spiritual Life*, trans. P. McNulty, Faber and Faber, 1959

De Jaegher, P., *The Virtue of Trust*, Burns, Oates and Washbourne, 1931

Flanagan, D., *In Praise of Mary*, Veritas, 1975

Foucauld, Charles de, *Meditations of a Hermit*, trans. C. Balfour, Burns, Oates and Washbourne, 1930

Francis de Sales, St, *Treatise on the Love of God*, trans. V. Kerns, Burns and Oates, 1962

Francis, St, *Francis and Clare: Complete Works*, St Paul, 1982

Garonne, G., *The Nun, Sacrament of God's Saving Presence*, Alba House, 1967

Guardini, R., *The Rosary of Our Lady*, Longman's Green, 1957

Hildegard of Bingen, *Meditations*, trans. G. Uhlen, Bear and Co., 1983

Houselander, Caryll, *The Reed of God*, Sheed and Ward, 1948

John of the Cross, St, *Complete Works*, trans. D. Lewis, Longman Green, 1864

John XXIII, Pope, *Journal of a Soul*, trans. D. White, Geoffrey Chapman, 1964

John Paul II, Pope, *Redemptionis Mater*, CTS, 1987

Julian of Norwich, *Revelations of Divine Love*, trans. J. Pichler (unpublished)

Laurentin, R., *Bernadette of Lourdes*, trans. J. Drury, DLT, 1979

Leen, E., *In the Likeness of Christ*, Sheed and Ward, 1936

Lynch, M., *Aylesford Newsletters*, published by Aylesford Shrine

Marmion, Dom C., *Christ in His Mysteries*, trans. by a Nun of Tyburn Convent, Sands and Co., 1925

Marmion, Dom C., *Christ the Life of the Soul*, trans. by a Nun of Tyburn Convent, Sands and Co., 1925

Newman, J. H., *Meditations and Devotions*, Longman's Green, 1953

O'Connell, Sir J. R., *Lyra Martyrum*, Burns, Oates and Washbourne, 1934

Patsch, J., *Our Lady in the Gospels*, Burns and Oates, 1958

Paul IV, Pope, *Marialis Cultus*, CTS, 1974

Philipon, M., *The Spiritual Doctrine of Sr Elizabeth of the Trinity*, trans. by a Nun of Stanbrook, Mercier Press, 1947

Rahner, K., *Mary, Mother of the Lord*, Anthony Clark, 1963

Regue, R., *Father Marie Eugene Grialou*, private printing, undated

Sheed, F., *The Mary Book*, Sheed and Ward, 1950

Sophrony, Archimandrite, *Wisdom from Mount Athos*, trans. R. Edmonds, St Vladimir Seminary Press, 1975

Stackpoole, A. (ed.), *Mary's Place in Christian Dialogue*, St Paul, 1982

Teresa of Avila, *Complete Works*, trans. E. Allison Peers, Sheed and Ward, 1945

Thérèse of Lisieux, St, *Poems*, trans. D. Kinney, ICS Publications, 1996